Sweden

THE WELFARE STATE

Sweden

THE WELFARE STATE

Wilfrid Fleisher

ILLUSTRATED

The John Day Company
New York

*This book is dedicated to
an experiment in democracy*

Contents

Illustrations

Foreword

THIS is a reporter's story—a factual account of the efforts of a small country to evolve an ideal pattern of life for its people. It is written as objectively as possible, for I have no ax to grind other than perhaps the thought that we in the United States might have something to learn from the Swedish example. I have made few comparisons because I realize that what is applicable to one country may not be at all suitable to another where entirely different conditions prevail. History, geography, and economics render such comparisons almost futile.

The idea to write this book came to me when I was press attaché at the American Embassy in Stockholm. Thousands of Americans visit Sweden every summer. Hundreds came to the Embassy. Most of them had heard that Sweden was far advanced in welfare and provided something of a model for the rest of the world. Successive Congressional committees also visited Sweden to study the co-operatives, housing, the medical program, and labor problems. This book is my answer to their many questions.

I have not been content only to talk with those officials who have to do with the administration of the Swedish welfare program. I have been far more interested in those whom this program has affected—the businessman, the worker, the farmer, the sick, the young, the aged, the prisoner—in other words, men and women in all ranks and at all levels of society. I looked for average and typical examples, but it was not long before I came to the conclusion that there is no average in the realm of human affairs: misery, poverty, and suffering have no set pattern and there is no single way to deal with them.

When I had completed this manuscript, I showed it to two prominent Swedish political leaders of opposite party affiliation. The Social Democrat commented that he considered it "harmful" to the party cause. The Conservative found that I had given "too much credit" to the Social Democrats. From these remarks, I concluded that I had attained my aim of being completely objective.

I have figured the exchange of the Swedish crown, in keeping with the official rate, at the round figure of five to the U.S. dollar. I am quite aware that this does not provide an accurate comparison in costs and that it gives a somewhat false impression that living in Sweden is cheaper than it actually is. It is cheaper at certain levels and more expensive at others. Economists figure that the exchange, in terms of the average cost of living, should be somewhere between two and three crowns to the dollar.

In preparing this book, I was fortunate to have the help of several unusually capable research assistants. Helen Lindahl was able to put me into contact with a number of cases to illustrate the workings of the welfare program, and her own knowledge of social conditions in Sweden was invaluable; Mrs. Karna Lagerkvist, a resourceful member of the Norwegian underground during the last world war, made a very thorough and expert study of various phases of the program; Madeleine Unnerstad was hard-working and helpful; and Mrs. Nyberg Larsson assisted me with some of the most complicated research and cleverly pieced together the tangled background of the development of Sweden's iron-ore trade. My thanks are also due to several hundred persons, officials and others, whom I interviewed, some of whom are listed elsewhere. It is said that Swedes are reticent, particularly in discussing their own affairs, but I was received everywhere most cordially, and people spoke to me frankly and without reserve of their problems, often very personal ones. No one could expect more co-operation than I obtained.

WILFRID FLEISHER

Stockholm

Sweden

THE WELFARE STATE

The Labor Movement

SWEDEN is known as the welfare state. Her own politicians have dubbed their country "the People's Home." The Swedish way of life is a unique experiment, evolved to meet the requirements of a small, homogeneous, democratic land. It is not based on any ideology in the sense that there is a dogma to be fulfilled, but has been worked out to meet specific conditions as they arise in an attempt to banish poverty and to provide a decent standard of living for all the people.

Such a program would not have been possible if Sweden had not been richly endowed with natural resources which the ingenuity and skill of her people have turned into production and, mainly, into exports. The labor party claims the credit for much of what has been accomplished, but while the Social Democratic Party championed the rights of the workers, the welfare program has become a reality because industry and business have developed the potential wealth of the country and provided the wherewithal. No poor country could have afforded it.

The welfare program grew along with the labor movement, which gave it its impetus and promoted its development. The rise of labor was rapid, steady, and orderly. It took a little over forty years for the labor party to come to power, and it has held that power with only brief interruptions for the past quarter of a century. Swedish labor leaders stress that their party attained its dominant position by constitutional means, and with a complete absence of violence. If it was a revolution it was a peaceful one, typical of the sturdy, unemotional character and temperament of the people.

The industrial revolution reached Sweden belatedly in the latter part of the last century, bringing with it unemployment and famine. As a result hundreds of thousands of Swedes emigrated to the United States to seek their fortune in the land of promise. It was against this background that the socialist editor Hjalmar Branting emerged as the pioneer of the Swedish labor movement. In a speech which he delivered to workers in 1886, regarded by historians as the first platform of the labor party, he urged the workers to organize a political party to press for labor reforms by a peaceful remodeling of society.

The Social Democratic Party was born three years later. All labor unions were invited to join in the political movement, and the party and the unions have worked hand in hand ever since. In the last election in 1954, two-thirds of the Social Democratic vote came from members of the powerful Swedish Confederation of Trade Unions (LO). The party organization is carried on through labor communes established throughout the country, and party membership may be individual or pledged through local trade unions and party clubs in factories and working places.

One of Branting's first aims was to bring about manhood suffrage. The Parliament had earlier been composed of classes—nobility, clergy, burghers, and peasants. It had been replaced by an elected chamber, but candidates and voters were limited to those with a fixed income higher than the average laborer's. This restriction had the effect of barring most workers from politics. There followed a thirty-year struggle before popular suffrage was achieved. The immediate effect was to give the labor party a substantial representation in Parliament. Branting was the first labor member elected to Parliament and the first Prime Minister of a labor government in Sweden.

Shortly after Branting's death in 1925 the power passed to Per Albin Hansson, another party stalwart. Gustav Möller, a contemporary of both who held the key post of Minister of Social Welfare over twenty years, never developed the forceful leadership of his two colleagues, but he was the party Santa Claus who conceived many of the welfare projects and carried them out. Tage Erlander, the present Prime Minister, took over unexpectedly when Per Albin died in 1946, and he is now the party head. But if Erlander was at first the façade for the leadership rather than the source of power, he has since grown into his role as politician and statesman.

As a newspaperman I have interviewed all four leaders. I well remember the square-shouldered, heavy-set figure of Branting, in an unpressed suit with baggy knees, when he was at the League of Nations in Geneva during the early twenties. The tall, ponderous, slow-moving Swede with the gray bushy hair and long curling mustache was a familiar figure among delegates. He was a visionary who preached peace to a war-weary forum, but he was not a pacifist: he strongly opposed those elements within his own party who urged a slackening of Sweden's defense. He believed in disarmament only if it should become universal.

I met Per Albin Hansson only a few days before his death. My interview had to be postponed an hour because he had been taken ill. He probably had suffered the first of the heart attacks which were to claim his life so soon. I found the short, stubby, baldheaded man, somewhat sharp in manner and very determined. It was at a time when Sweden was about to enter into a much discussed billion crown ($200,000,000) trade pact with the Soviet Union. The United States had delivered a protest and I was anxious to hear what Per Albin had to say about it. He brushed my question peremptorily aside. He made it plain that he considered it none of America's business and, what was more, none of my business either. He refused to discuss the subject further or to be led back to it. The rest of our conversation, after an embarrassing pause, was devoted to internal problems, of which there were many at the time, for although Sweden had emerged prosperous from the war that raged all around her, there were all kinds of shortages, particularly fuel, and the people were restless.

It was obvious that Per Albin was a man of strong will and that he followed his own course. It was this dogged, staunch attitude which earned him the confidence of the people in the war days when, along with the late King Gustav V, he firmly adhered to a policy of neutrality for Sweden. His radio addresses to the country lent encouragement when there was, in fact, little basis for it in view of Sweden's unpreparedness in the early part of the conflict.

His death was typical of the simplicity in which he had always lived. He had attended an official dinner in honor of the visiting Norwegian Prime Minister and was returning by streetcar to his home in a poor suburb. He dropped dead as he stepped off the streetcar and was found by astonished passers-by who recognized at once the prostrate form of the popular Prime Minister.

A week later I stood precariously on the top of a high pile of wooden logs which lined the streets of Stockholm in the postwar days—Sweden's reserve of fuel for the coming winter, a subject which Per Albin had discussed with so much concern when we met—and watched the mournful procession as the coffin of the little man was borne to its last resting place, followed by thousands of plain, sorrowful, tearful people. As one man remarked to me, "He was the father of the People's Home."

Perhaps no one was more surprised than Tage Erlander himself when he succeeded Per Albin as Prime Minister. He had been an inconspicuous member of the party, mainly interested in academic matters. He had long been editor of a popular encyclopedia and had become head of the Board of Education. He had no ambition or desire to become a national leader. He was overwhelmed and ill at ease.

The story is told that when Erlander took the oath of office in the presence of the late King Gustav V, he hesitated to place two fingers on the Bible in the traditional manner, saying that he did not believe much in God. The King, who was standing close by, is said to have remarked, "I don't see why you should worry, perhaps He doesn't believe too much in you."

The incident is typical of the hesitation with which Erlander approached his task as head of both the Government and his party. I first interviewed him just after he had taken office, following long, arduous days of party meetings. I had an appointment to meet him in the Chancery—Government House. I wandered about the long empty corridors unescorted, poking my head into one office after another. Eventually I came upon a tall, awkward, tired-looking man leaning over a desk in an office by himself. I asked him to direct me to the Prime Minister. He rose, shook hands, and said, "That's me."

Erlander talked with a certain nostalgia. He seemed to regret leaving his academic career behind him. He had been busy, he explained, sponsoring a new educational reform program which, among other things, would make it compulsory to study more English in the schools. He would have liked to see this program through, but now he must pass the work on to others.

From the outset, Erlander demonstrated a surprising ease in public speaking and agility in debate which, coupled with a dry sense of humor, promised well for a politician. As a platform speaker and in election campaigns he could measure up to any opponent. He was best when speaking off the cuff, and he seemed able to turn any argument to his advantage. With experience he has gained considerable assurance and lost the shy, embarrassed manner which marked his early appearances. He is now fully at ease, a polished, confident politician, conscious of his position and of the responsibility he bears.

When he came to power Erlander found a ready-made party platform. The aims of the labor party had been incorporated in a twenty-seven-point program drawn up in 1944 when it seemed that the war was close to an end and that it would be followed by a depression. The principal authors of the program were Ernst Wigfors and Richard Sterner, both left-wing Social Democrats. The program stressed that the party's chief objective was to maintain full employment no matter what happened. "No able-bodied man or woman," it declared, "should suffer enforced idleness any longer than is necessary to change from one occupation to another or to undergo training or retraining." It called upon the Government to encourage the export industry; promote agriculture by loans and subsidies; carry out an extensive housing program; and undertake public works. It proposed that the Government should combat business "monopolies" by entering into competition either directly or through "nonprofit organizations," meaning the co-operatives. It urged that the State take over any industry which might become too powerful, and it called specifically for the nationalization of coal and oil imports.

In addition, the program called for a long list of new benefits: higher pay for farmers to bring their income up to that of industrial workers; extension of unemployment insurance to cover all workers; shorter working hours and longer vacations; compulsory universal health insurance providing for both hospital and medical care; increased maternity benefits to reduce the number of abortions; higher pensions for old age, invalids, the blind, and other special categories; better facilities for higher education, with the eventual goal of compulsory schooling for nine or ten years instead of seven or eight; the opening up of more jobs for women; equal pay for men and women for similar work; a leveling of wealth by taxation; and a limitation on large private estates.

As in the case of most party platforms, many of the proposals have since been discarded or have become obsolete, particularly those relating to labor and industry. The depression which was envisaged never materialized: to the contrary, business has boomed and Sweden has had an uninterrupted era of prosperity with full or overfull employment.

Premier Erlander insists that the party has not surrendered any of its principles, but he points out that the program was intended to be a five-year plan and that over the past decade conditions have changed and some of the provisions have become unnecessary. This is only partially true. The fact is that the Social Democratic Party itself has not fared too well. It reached the peak of its power during World War II when Per Albin Hansson was at the height of his popularity and the party had a clear majority in both houses of Parliament, but it began to lose ground toward the end of the war once Sweden felt secure again. It suffered a further setback in the first postwar election in 1948, when the main campaign issue was increased socialization—advocated by the Social Democrats—as against an end to it—demanded by the opposition parties. This caused the Government to slow down in its experimentation. Since then the labor party has lost more strength and no longer has a majority in the lower house. This has forced the Social Democrats into a coalition with the Farmers' Party, which has been given four of the sixteen cabinet posts. Because the agrarians are conservative they have had the effect of a further brake on socialization.

The Social Democratic Party itself has backtracked on some of its demands. At its congress in 1952 the party declared that "no total nationalization of industry is aimed at, even at a distant date. Private enterprise will always hold a sector of commerce, industry, and handicrafts."

Premier Erlander amplified this statement when he said to me, "Some things have been set aside. We have not been interested in nationalization for its own sake, but only to obtain very concrete and substantial objectives."

Prosperous times, however, have enabled the Government to fulfill most of its promises with regard to welfare benefits. Social Democrats were particularly pleased with the legislative program enacted by the 1952 session of Parliament, which they refer to as "the Parliament of the great reforms." It passed long-pending legislation for compulsory health insurance, which came into effect on January 1, 1955. It also approved substantial increases for old-age pensions, one of the benefits of the welfare program upon which the greatest stress has been laid, and an extension of unemployment insurance. The Government, with the approval of Parliament, extended the two-week compulsory summer vacation for all workers to seventeen days, and to three weeks after 1956. Furthermore, a commission was appointed to make recommendations for the equalization of women's pay.

The foreign policy of the Social Democratic Party can be summarized in the word "neutrality," but the party prefers to call it "freedom from alliance." This policy has the support of all political parties and the overwhelming endorsement of the Swedish people, who are determined, if possible, to stay out of another world conflict as they did in the last two world wars. Few Swedes, however, have any illusions on this subject or believe this can be done, but they are unwilling to throw away the chance, no matter how slim, in advance.

The Swedish Government contends that it was willing to abandon the traditional neutrality policy that has kept Sweden out of war for 142 years when it offered to take part in a defense agreement with Norway and Denmark in 1948, before the Atlantic Pact was concluded. But this offer was conditional upon members of this Nordic bloc remaining free from outside alliances and can just as well be regarded as an attempt to extend Sweden's neutrality to her Scandinavian neighbors. The Swedish explanation for not joining in the Atlantic Pact was that she was fearful Russia would take over Finland, and the Russian frontier would be moved up to Sweden's own border. This is an argument that can never be proved or disproved.

The Swedes feel that their policy of neutrality has been justified and that it has brought them unexpected prestige. They were reluctant but flattered to participate in the Armistice and Repatriation commissions in Korea, and they have never doubted that the selection of Dag Hammarskjöld as Secretary General of the United Nations was due to their country's neutral position. Premier Erlander has stated that there is need for a neutral state and that respect for Sweden has not been altered by the policy she has pursued. And Foreign Minister Östen Undén, one of the firmest believers in neutrality, has remarked with a touch of bitterness that "the world may have use for neutral countries in certain situations, contrary to what some people believe." Sweden's role as intermediary in Peking, even if only as a messenger, is regarded as proof that a divided world may have good use for the few neutrals that exist.

Sweden's neutrality, however, is not a strictly middle-of-the-road one but has a Western slant in conformity with public opinion, which is historically anti-Russian and leans sentimentally toward the Western nations, whose democratic ideals are shared by the Swedish people. It is inconceivable that Sweden should ever willingly be aligned with Russia in any conflict. Sweden's defense plans are directed against an attack from the east, and are based on the hope, if not the belief, that in such an event Sweden would find support from the Western nations. Sweden has not neglected her own defense. By the end of the last world war she had built up her armaments to such an extent that any aggressor would have had to reckon with the consequences, and she has since maintained and improved her equipment. She has now the fourth largest air force in the world, following the United States, Russia and Britain. She can mobilize an army of over a half a million men at short notice in the event of war, and she has built several hundred underground shelters, deep in granite rock, for military and civil defense.

Neutrality is characteristic of the mind of the Swedish people, who take a passive attitude in most matters. It is as typical of Sweden as the long, drab, gray winter days or the gray material which adorns the women in the streets of Stockholm. The thoughts of the people are turned inward and are focused on their own problems, detached from events of the outside world. It is this outlook which has perhaps caused the Swedes to place so much emphasis on their own welfare that they have made it the main item in their national budget.

The Social Democratic Party is against Communism, but it has not always been so. There was a period after the last war when the Social Democrats were satisfied to have the Communists in Parliament vote with them to give them the edge they needed for a safe majority. But this tacit arrangement came to an abrupt end after the Communist coup in Czechoslovakia and the Russian so-called Mutual Assistance Pact with Finland brought home to the Swedish people the real danger of Communism.

The Swedish attitude toward Communism until then had been a tolerant one. The Communist Party was looked upon as a political entity rather than a subversive movement. The policy was to let the Communists have their say, in the belief that an informed public would reject and condemn Communist methods, rather than attempt to suppress the movement which, it was feared, might thus be driven underground. Premier Erlander explained the Government's policy in 1948 as follows: "We have carried on the fight against Communism in the way that it should be carried on in a democracy—by means of information." In accordance with that policy, he himself appeared in a public debate in Stockholm's Concert House with the then Communist leader, Linderoth, and he refuted the Communist arguments on foreign and domestic policy point by point.

But both Erlander and his party have since changed their policy and tactics. The Stockholm Peace Appeal, launched on orders from Moscow, contributed largely to this change. It became apparent to the Government and to the Swedish people that their country was being made the dupe of the Communists before the whole world. Erlander declared then that "it is with a feeling of strong disgust that we Swedes witness the brandishing of our capital's name in this way in international Communist propaganda. Actually this so-called Stockholm appeal has no more connection with Stockholm or Sweden than earlier appeals, emanating from so-called

peace conferences in Paris and New York, represented democratic opinions in France and the United States."

And in May, 1950, Erlander officially declared war on the
Communist Party when he told the Parliament, "I wish to
make it quite clear that the party I represent does not hesi-
tate to characterize the Swedish Communist Party as representative of an ideology alien and hostile to our democratic
order. It can count on us only as its enemy."

If anything further was needed to discredit the Communists, successive spy trials in which Swedish Communists were
involved as agents of Moscow aroused nation-wide hostility.
The people learned to their dismay that a very substantial part of their military secrets, including their northern and coastal fortifications, were known to the Russians,
necessitating a revision of their defense plans at tremendous
cost. Later attempts to shift espionage activities to satellite
diplomats and their stooges made matters no better.

It is no wonder therefore that the Swedish Communist
Party has steadily lost support. Communist strength reached
its peak in the election of 1946, when the party polled 11.2
per cent of the electorate, a total of 372,242 votes. Since then
it has dropped off in the elections held every two years, and
fell to 4.9 per cent in the last election in 1954 with 182,576
votes. Communist strength has also dwindled in the trade
unions, which were heavily infiltrated, and is currently almost negligible.

The Swedish Government is now alive to the Communist
threat from within. It realizes how dangerous a fifth column
could be in northern Sweden where Communists have been
the strongest. This is the sensitive area that borders on Finland, and the most exposed in the event of an overland attack
from the east. It contains valuable iron ore mines, some of
the country's largest ironworks and the biggest power plants
supplying electricity to virtually the entire country. It is ob-

vious what enormous damage even a single worker could do by way of sabotage in this strategic area. For this reason, the Government has been compiling lists of known and suspected Communists who could be quickly rounded up and interned in the event of war.

Since Sweden has a predominantly labor government, it is natural that the chairman of LO, the Confederation of Trade Unions, should be a man of great influence. This position is now held by sixty-three-year-old Axel Strand, who speaks for 1,360,000 workers. In Sweden the percentage of workers who are members of trade unions in relation to the total population is higher than that of any other country in the world. One in every five Swedes belongs to a trade union, as compared to one in every ten Americans.

Strand's manner is not what might be expected of a labor leader, or of a man who must appeal to the working masses. On the contrary, he is quiet, calm, unobtrusive, and a far better listener than speaker. He is genial and friendly, but it is his straightforwardness and refusal to enter into intrigue that have earned him the confidence of his fellow workers. When Strand speaks the Government listens, not only because he represents the labor force but because he usually has something constructive to offer.

In his office at LO headquarters Strand sits complacently at a large desk, puffing a cigar and toying with a paperknife. Callers are many, but few are admitted, and his telephone is answered by a staff of secretaries in an outer office. In meetings with labor leaders and others, Strand sits and listens patiently, injecting only an occasional remark, but when he does it carries great weight.

Born the son of a carpenter in a southern village in Sweden, Axel Strand, following in his father's footsteps, became a skilled cabinetmaker. He moved to Stockholm as a young man to pursue his trade and there joined the Woodworkers'

Federation, his first contact with a labor union. It was not long before his colleagues chose this silent, self-effacing, plodding worker as chairman of their union. Strand, quick to realize that he needed more education than the elementary schooling he had received, subscribed to a series of correspondence courses, including bookkeeping, accounting, and languages. It was this knowledge of economics which later qualified him for the post of treasurer of LO, which he held for ten years before becoming its chairman in 1947. He is now a member of Parliament and is the Social Democratic Party leader and Deputy Speaker in the First Chamber.

According to Einar Norrman, a former vice chairman of LO, the two distinguishing features of the Swedish labor movement are the collective wage agreements and the labor court. Besides LO, which embraces almost all workers in Swedish industries, there is the Salaried Employees' Association, known as TCO, which includes most white-collar workers. Management long ago organized in self-defense, establishing the Employers' Federation, SAF, which represents 11,600 employers. Collective agreements are negotiated between these groups, employers on the one hand and workers on the other. These agreements, usually good for one year, provide for automatic increases in pay when the cost-of-living index reaches certain levels. They are binding on both management and labor for their duration, and strikes and lockouts are permissible only after they expire. No union is allowed to strike without the consent of LO if the strike involves more than 3 per cent of the union's membership.

Under Swedish law, the Government appoints professional conciliators to bring the parties together in labor disputes. Differences regarding the interpretation of collective agreements come before a special labor court which acts as a compulsory board of arbitration and which may award damages. As a result of the collective agreements and the methods for conciliation, there have been very few strikes in Sweden within the past decade. The only major strike occurred among metalworkers in 1945 after the end of the war, a conflict which was fanned by the Communists and lasted five months, involving over a million men.

Strand stands by the platform of the Social Democratic Party. He wants full employment, a higher standard of living for the workers, and what he and the party call "increased economic democracy." This means, Strand explains, that the so-called enterprise councils, consisting of representatives of management and labor now established in Swedish factories to discuss safety measures and working conditions, should be broadened to give labor a voice in problems of production.

Strand recognizes that the average Swedish worker is anxious to raise his standard of living but does not aim to "rise above his class." It is rare, he says, that a Swedish laborer seeks to become a white-collar worker or executive in a factory. Workers are even reluctant to become foremen within their own groups. The more ambitious workmen rise through the trade unions and go into politics. No political office is beyond their reach and many Government and party leaders have attained their positions in this manner.

There is perhaps no better illustration of the attitude of the average Swedish laborer than that revealed by a recent film sponsored by the Social Democratic Party for election purposes. The simple story of a worker and his family, it goes back to 1932 when Sweden was suffering from world depression. Andersson, the worker and hero of the picture, had been unemployed for over a year and was tramping about in the rain looking in vain for a job on the eve of the election that first brought the Social Democratic Party to power. His family attempted to persuade Andersson that the best way to overcome his troubles was to vote the Social Democratic ticket. He did so reluctantly, but almost immediately everything began to clear up. The rain stopped, the fog dissipated and the sun came out. Andersson obtained a relief job as a workman building roads. A slight romance was introduced into the picture when he fell in love with the daughter of an office worker. This was frowned upon by both families but they eventually married. Over a period of years Andersson was able to raise his standard of living due to the benefits he received from the Social Democratic regime, including assistance in erecting a prefabricated house, free hospitalization for his wife at childbirth, a child subsidy, low-cost medical care, old-age pension for his parents, and eventually a free burial for his father. At the end of the picture Andersson was still working as an ordinary laborer after eighteen years, but he seemed perfectly happy with the benefits which the party had provided, and he apparently had no ambition for advancement. The picture closed with everyone going out to vote for the Social Democratic Party in a new election.

To this American observer the film seemed to sell failure, since Andersson did not rise even as far as foreman, but this apparently did not disturb the thousands of Swedish workers to whom it was shown as labor party propaganda. The benefits were what counted.

There is a greater degree of employment security in Sweden than in most other countries. A job is frequently a lifetime one. In fact, nine out of ten Swedes employed in business remain with the same firm. This stability is not provided by law, although a discharged employee may appeal to the courts if he feels that he has been unfairly treated; nor is it the result of agreement with the trade unions or employee organizations, although they do play a role; it is largely a matter of custom and tradition.

No Swedish firm of good standing risks its reputation by summarily discharging an employee, particularly if he has been employed for a number of years. This places a heavy responsibility upon business executives in the selection of their staff, since they must bear in mind that a job may be a lifetime one and that the efficiency or ability of the employee is not a deciding factor. As a result, every Swedish firm has a certain amount of deadwood among its employees, an unavoidable burden.

Management has persistently held out for the right to discharge employees, and this principle has been recognized in all agreements with employees, with the reservation that no employer is allowed to dismiss a worker because he joins a labor union. The amount of notice that must be given to a discharged employee is stipulated in the central agreement between the Employers' Federation and the trade unions which serves as a model for all business relations. But there is a wide gap between the letter of the agreement and what actually takes place. In practice, an employer rarely discharges an employee of several years' standing unless he commits a very serious offense. Inefficiency, lack of ability, or a lack of interest in the work are not sufficient reasons for dismissal. They may influence an employee's advancement or may lead to premature retirement with pension, but these are risks which a firm must take if it retains an employee until his position has become established.

Banks, always very conservative, provide the maximum security for their employees. The Skandinaviska Bank, Sweden's second largest banking institution, gives a two- or three-year training course to young men and women entering its service. During that period they are on trial. But once they have qualified as regular employees they cannot be discharged except in cases of grave misconduct. Most bank employees fulfill their thirty-five-year term of service until they are pensioned. Those who show less aptitude do not advance as rapidly, and in some few cases special jobs have to be created for those who are entitled to automatic promotion by length of service but do not qualify for the higher positions. This same condition holds true for all reputable firms and business establishments.

Certain categories of Government employees in the middle brackets cannot be dismissed without a court ruling, and they, in turn, cannot resign and are frozen in their jobs. These are the more highly paid civil servants who have reached their positions through long years of routine service to the State, but who are not executives. It is reckoned that they have earned steady employment with an assured pension and that they desire nothing else. Inasmuch as the Government operates most public utilities, this applies to certain railway workers, post-office, telegraph, and customs officials—the upper Government bureaucracy.

Women may not be dismissed because they marry or raise a family. Labor agreements stipulate that a woman is entitled to a six-month leave of absence during pregnancy, with a salary equaling approximately three-quarters of her pay. Even a domestic servant must be retained during pregnancy and for at least three months after the birth of the child.

An employee who feels that he has been unfairly dismissed may appeal to his trade union or organization, seek arbitration, or sue in court. Although such disputes are generally negotiated, a recent case of interest did reach the courts. It was that of a chemical engineer who had resigned from a firm to take a better job elsewhere. He was, however, discharged from the second job a year later. As he was over fifty years of age and had twice changed employment, he was unable to find work, and he sued his last employer, who was ordered by the court to pay his full salary up to the retirement age of sixty-five and its share of his pension from the time it employed him. There is no law to cover such cases. The courts are guided by "current practice."

While employment is remarkably stable, it is surprising

to find that only a third of all salaried employees in Sweden are provided by their employers with retirement or life insurance. In the case of industrial workers even less provision is made, and only one laborer in six is insured by his firm. Most of the business insurance is handled by the Swedish Employers' Pension Fund, a nonprofit organization maintained by trade and industry to provide low-rate insurance for salaried employees. This insurance provides a retirement allowance after thirty years of service equal to 60 per cent of the beneficiary's salary, and also allots 30 per cent to widows of deceased employees, with slight increases for dependent minor children. For these benefits there is a pay-check deduction of as much as 6 per cent for single employees and 8 per cent for married workers. The employer contributes his share of the cost of insurance, which is double the amount put up by the employee.

This insurance is transferable only if the worker's next job is with another member of the Swedish Employers' Pension Fund. Otherwise, he receives only a fraction of the insurance due for the years he has been employed. Firms not associated with the fund which have their own pension plans usually pay a lump sum on retirement at the age of sixty-seven if the worker has been employed for over ten or fifteen years. This makes it extremely difficult for older workers to find employment, since many firms are reluctant to take on employees to whom they must pay a retirement allowance after a relatively short term of service.

Recognizing the shortcomings of the pension system, the Government has drawn up a scheme for compulsory insurance which, if approved by the Parliament, would come into effect in 1958. Every Swede would be enrolled and would receive a pension upon reaching the age of sixty-seven, amounting to 36 per cent of his average income during his gainful years. To make this possible, every citizen between the ages of seventeen and sixty-four would pay a premium on his earnings and whatever other income he might have up to a maximum of $6,000 total annual income. The premium would start at 2.5 per cent and gradually be increased to 8 per cent. Employers would pay half the premium on salaries. This pension would supplement the old-age pension to which all Swedes are now entitled, and, in the lowest income brackets, the two combined would even exceed the beneficiary's former income.

The development of the labor movement has, of course, made its impact upon the monarchy, but not to the extent contemplated by the party founders. The Social Democratic Party platform calls for a republic, but there is little likelihood that the party will press for a change so long as the present King remains on the throne and is able to carry out his functions. I asked Premier Erlander point-blank about the party's attitude toward a republic, and he replied, "If nothing extraordinary occurs, we are not going to raise the issue."

Periodically there has been a certain amount of agitation in favor of a republic. Several resolutions favoring a republic came before the party congress in the summer of 1952. They were sponsored by communes in and around Stockholm. The party board declared then that it found no reason to render an opinion but added that it would not oppose a discussion among party members as to what sort of a republic they might want. Richard Sandler, a former Foreign Minister and party leader, said the people should consider whether a republic should be modeled on the American presidential system, "with authority far beyond that of a Swedish constitutional monarch"; on the French system, with a president "whose power is approximately equal to a constitutional monarch in a parliamentary regime"; or on the Swiss pattern, with a president appointed in rotation for one year from among the members of the Government.

The republican movement has attracted increased attention recently with the organization of a Republican Club. The movement seems to have profited from three circumstances: reports of a homosexual scandal allegedly involving the late King Gustav V, which was revealed after his death; uncertainty about the succession due to a dangerous gap in ages between the present King, who is seventy-three, and the young Crown Prince, only nine years old; and renewed pressure from the more radical elements within the Social Democratic Party, who regard the monarchy as an outworn institution.

Much of the antiroyalist agitation can be traced to Vilhelm Moberg, author of several bestsellers on Swedish emigration to the United States, who has a flair for scandal. It was Moberg who gained access at police headquarters to the secret dossier in the so-called Haijby affair, a case of blackmail by an ex-convict named Kurt Haijby, who was alleged to have had personal relations with the old King. Moberg obtained photostatic copies of some of the documents, which passed into the hands of newspaper editors. The Government was apparently either unwilling or unable to suppress the demand for release of the Haijby report. Moberg left hurriedly for the United States just before the scandal broke and when justice authorities became anxious to know how he came upon the documents. It is his daughter, Eva Moberg, who is the leader of the newly formed Republican Club, to which her father promptly gave his support when he returned to Sweden for the inaugural meeting. In a newly published booklet, Moberg urges a republic on the Swiss pattern.

The issue of a republic is discussed openly and there seems to be no thought that it is treason, lese majesty, or even disloyal, so long as the change is advocated by orderly means and not by revolution or violence. Swedes are proud of the freedom that permits them to discuss all matters of public interest, and they show no hesitation about doing so. The most common thought is that if the question of a republic should someday become a live issue, the decision should be made by a plebiscite in which every voter would have the right to express himself.

The late King Gustav V was the first monarch to have to deal with a socialist government, and he did so with rare adroitness. He cleverly steered a middle-of-the-road course, sacrificing as little as possible of the royal prerogatives while conforming to changing circumstances sufficiently to meet socialist requirements. It was no easy task to strike such a balance, but he succeeded by giving very little away. Over a long reign of forty-three years—the longest in Swedish history —he gained a position that was unshakable and that better enabled him to preserve the royal prestige. He retained his dignity at all times. He felt that respect was due him as a royal personage, as sovereign, and as head of the State, and he expected it from his court, his cabinet, and his people.

From the very outset Gustav V showed that he would exact respect from the socialists. At his first meeting with his socialist cabinet he found upon entering the council chamber that the members had remained seated, apparently in silent protest against the monarchy. The King, with a detached air, looked around and remarked audibly, "I must be too early, there doesn't seem to be anyone here," and walked out. When he returned ten minutes later the entire cabinet rose from their seats. It was a lesson they never had to be taught again.

Gustav V understood, perhaps better than anyone else, the limitations of his office as constitutional monarch, and he only intervened in matters of policy in times of grave crisis. He is said to have been his own best foreign minister, and is credited with having kept his country out of two world wars.

Whether he actually threatened to abdicate during World War II if the German demand for the transfer of a Nazi division from Norway to Finland over Swedish territory was not granted is a matter of historical debate, but it is believed that he gave a very strong hint that he considered this course necessary if Sweden was to stay out of the war.

The men of the Swedish royal family seem to have found the secret of longevity. King Gustav V lived to the age of ninety-two, and he and his three brothers, to a total of three hundred sixty years. Many Swedes say he lived too long. Certainly no human being could be expected to retain all his faculties intact at that advanced age.

But, above all, the late King was a man of strong will and determination. I had an opportunity to judge of this at first hand when, as correspondent for the Columbia Broadcasting System, I interviewed him on the occasion of his ninetieth birthday, and he recorded a message for the American people.

When I arrived at Drottningholm Palace in the outskirts of Stockholm, where the King was then staying, I was informed by Grand Chamberlain Baron von Essen that the King was not well that day and might not be able to make the broadcast. However, a few minutes later the King appeared, walking with a cane. He crossed the room directly and sat down in a tapestried armchair before an antique desk on which the microphone had been placed. A short script had been written out for him in letters an inch high in order that he might read it easily. It was divided in two parts, about half in English, the remainder in Swedish, and addressed especially to Swedes in the United States.

Then, just as the aged monarch was about to speak into the microphone, he was taken with a violent coughing spell. It was a terrible cough with a long wheeze that shook his emaciated frame. However, the King recovered almost instantly and without a moment's hesitation again began reading the script. The radio technicians, who had disconnected the microphone to avoid recording the cough, were taken by surprise and missed the opening remarks, so that it was necessary for Sven Norberg, an official of the station, to interrupt the King. He did so apologetically, explaining that there had been some technical difficulty. The King, obviously irritated, turned and inquired, "Do I have to do it over again?"

"If Your Majesty would be so kind," murmured the embarrassed Norberg.

The King then started again to read the script in a low, deep but steady voice and had reached the end of the English section when he was taken with another and even worse coughing spell. He fell back in his chair, his arms limp by his side, and gasped, "I can't . . . do . . . any more."

He had, I thought, collapsed in making a superlative effort to broadcast to the American people—for me. Beads of sweat stood out on my brow. The seconds seemed like minutes as the monarch lay motionless in his chair. Then suddenly, as if by a miracle, he revived. He pulled himself together, sat erect, straightened his tie, adjusted his glasses, and inquired, "Do I have to do it over again?"

Once more Norberg stepped forward and said, "If Your Majesty will start in with the Swedish text I am sure it will be all right." The King then read the Swedish part slowly but surely to the end without faltering and in a voice that showed no trace of the ordeal he had just been through. "Let me now send you my personal greetings," he read, "and thank you for having, through your achievements and your efforts in your new country, enhanced Sweden's honor and fair name. God bless you all!"

When he had finished, he turned to me and inquired, "Was it all right?"

I heard myself mumbling, "It was very kind of Your

Majesty." I could say no more. It had been one of the most painful experiences in my career as a newspaperman.

The King rose from his chair, shook hands with each one of us, and left the room. Later, Baron von Essen asked me, "How did you find His Majesty?"

I answered, "Worse than I had expected."

"Oh, that was nothing," said the Baron, "he's always like that nowadays."

But if I retain one dominant impression of that memorable broadcast, it was the unflinching determination of King Gustav to carry out what he had set his mind to do. He was determined to make that broadcast, no matter what happened, even if the words were to be his last.

When the new king, Gustav VI Adolph, came to the throne in 1950, he took as his motto "duty before all," and no one who knows him can doubt that it was his own choice. While the old monarch had carried out his functions in a routine manner, except when major problems required his attention, the present King insists upon being informed in detail about all matters that come before him. Cabinet members who had looked upon the royal signature as a mere formality have learned that the King regards his consent as more than perfunctory. Not infrequently an embarrassed minister has been ordered to inform himself more fully and report back to the sovereign. Some ministers feel that the King carries this practice too far in view of his position as constitutional monarch. It is this great attention to detail that is said to have caused Premier Erlander to remark that whereas the old King needed only half a Prime Minister, the present one could use two.

It might be thought that the Swedish people would have been well acquainted with their new King through his many years of apprenticeship, but his role had been so self-effacing, in the shadow of the old King who always claimed the spotlight, that the people did not know what to expect of him. They have now learned that Gustav VI Adolph is solid, dependable, serious, hard-working, and even meticulous. These are qualities to be highly valued, particularly in a troubled world, although they may not appeal to the popular imagination. The King is conservative in his habits. He never touches alcohol, drinks barley water with a touch of lemon to give it flavor, and he never smokes.

The new King has shown that he is even more conscious than was his father of the changing times, and of the need for the monarchy to be democratic. Gustav V dispensed with a coronation after Sweden's separation from Norway because he was reluctant to acknowledge the limitation of his sovereignty in so public a manner. The present King followed the example of his father simply because he felt that a coronation was unnecessary.

One of the first acts of the new King was to abolish an old custom which required women to wear special court dress at palace functions. This was a black velvet gown with puffed sleeves and white lace collar and cuffs, which the King felt was an unnecessary expense and no longer in fashion. Women now attend court functions in evening dress.

A member of Parliament from a northern province once wrote to the King to inquire whether he was compelled to wear a dress suit at a state banquet at the palace, explaining that he did not possess one. The King personally replied, "Come as you are." This soon became a standard joke, and later the title of a popular revue.

The King may often be seen walking in the streets of Stockholm or shopping without a bodyguard. Sometimes he is accompanied by the Queen, British-born former Lady Louise Mountbatten, and she may have a lady-in-waiting along. The royal couple are familiar figures, recognized by everyone, but passers-by do not stop and stare at them. The Swed-

ish people want their royal family to behave like anyone else,
and they want them to feel at ease.

I have met the King on several occasions and heard him
discuss a variety of subjects ranging from art to the monarchy. He looks upon his role as that of the first servant of
the State—a job to be fulfilled faithfully like any other public
office. It is an arduous job, but he finds time occasionally for
relaxation and his hobbies, which include archaeology, art,
fishing, and gardening. It is said that had he not been King,
he might have been a professor of archaeology. His knowledge is not limited to books, for he has excavated in Greece,
Cyprus, and China, and few men know as much as he does
about early ceramics. His Chinese collection is world re-
nowned. But his interests are broader and he values Swedish modern art, personally encouraging young artists by visiting their exhibitions and purchasing their works. Several
times a week he manages to slip away from his official duties
for a game of tennis and is rated a better player than his
father was, although this is not generally known.

The King realizes, as his father did, that the position of
constitutional monarch has its limitations. He does not feel
that it gives him any particular influence other than that
which he can exert in a personal way. He goes along with his
Government no matter what kind of a cabinet it may be
politically. He maintains close contact with his ministers,
considering that a part of his duty. He believes, above all,
that in a democracy the royal family must behave in a democratic manner.

Some royalists and members of the nobility complain that
the King has gone too far in adopting democratic ways, and
that he ought to retain what little is left of the royal pomp
customarily associated with monarchy. But he feels that while
some measure of dignity belongs to his office, the broad
masses want him to be—as some Social Democrats express it—

something akin to a "royal president." Many Swedes declare
that if there should be a republic, they would vote for Gustav
VI Adolph as the first president.

The problem of the succession became acute when Prince
Gustav Adolph, eldest son of the King, was killed in an air-
plane crash in 1947, along with the American singer Grace
Moore. The young Crown Prince may not ascend the throne
until he reaches twenty-one years of age, Parliament having
recently increased the age from nineteen. This means that
unless the present King retains the throne until he is eighty-
five, in 1968, there will have to be a regency.

The law provides that Parliament shall appoint a regent,
or a regency council of three or five members. It is supposed
that a council would be preferable, and that its principal
members would be Prince Bertil, the only son of the King
who has not married a commoner, the Grand Marshal of the
Court, and the Prime Minister. The German-born Princess
Sibylla, mother of the Crown Prince, might be added by special act of Parliament. The risk is that if a regency proved unpopular, it might mean the end of the monarchy.

The Crown Prince, fondly known as the "little prince,"
is a picture-book child with curly blond hair, deep blue eyes,
and dimples. He is bright, alert, full of fun, and at times
even philosophical, as when he remarked upon awakening
after an operation for appendicitis, "Well, that was the worst
experience I ever had." His photographs appear frequently
in the newspapers and magazines, showing him playing with
one or more of his four older sisters, known as the Haga
princesses.

He is now a pupil at a fashionable private school in Stockholm. The teachers call him "Prince," and the children are
urged to do the same, but they have made up a nickname of
their own and call him *Knorpen,* a childish contraction of
the Swedish for "Crown Prince." I have watched young Carl

Gustav at play and at his weekly gymnastic lesson, his favorite hour. He is quicker than anyone else. When the teacher shouts, "Back to your places," he is there ahead of all the others.

The Crown Prince is being put through his paces carefully to prepare him eventually for the role of monarch, but whether Carl Gustav will ever ascend the ancient throne of "the Swedes, the Goths, and the Wends" as Carl XVI, no one can say.

CHAPTER II

Government and Big Business

THE welfare state is paternalistic, and while the bulk of Swedish industry is still in private hands, the Government controls many of the public utilities and some of the most important sources of production. Much of the nationalization took place before the socialists came to power, but the policy is being continued, although not as actively as the more radical members of the Social Democratic Party would like it to be.

The State operates the postal service, telegraph, telephone, most of the railways, nearly half of the bus lines, is a part owner in the Scandinavian Airlines System, and shares in the development of Sweden's three main resources: iron ore, forests, and water power. There has been talk of nationalizing the timber industry, insurance, banking, and the production of electrical and medical supplies, but there is no indication that the Government actually plans such steps. Nationalization is a policy held in reserve, to be brought forward whenever the Government finds it expedient. It hangs like the sword of Damocles over the heads of big enterprise.

At present 90 per cent of the railways are owned and operated by the Government. When they were first built a century ago, the policy was that the Government would be responsible for the main lines and that branch lines would be in the hands of private enterprise. Since then the Government has gradually acquired most of the railways, as the branch lines are frequently the most profitable, particularly the ore railways. As for bus lines, 40 per cent are owned by the State, but shipping has been left virtually untouched under private ownership.

Price legislation is a powerful instrument of government control of industry; it enables the Government to fix retail prices, to set the price when the goods leave the factory, and to investigate, if need be, the producer's margin of profit. There is no antitrust law such as exists in the United States, nor is there likely to be, since the co-operatives enjoy Government favor; but the State has the authority to revoke a cartel agreement if it is considered harmful. There are also import and export restrictions, largely leftovers from the war and immediate postwar periods, which give the Government control over the country's foreign trade.

The Government and big business have worked out a relationship built on mutual dependence. The Government realizes that it needs the brains and ability of big business to turn Sweden's natural resources into production which makes the welfare state possible, while big business recognizes that, in order to succeed, it must have the support of the Government. This has produced an uneasy alliance, with big business in the role of plaintiff, but it is a workable one, and both sides are apparently determined to make the best of it.

It is a curious phenomenon in a socialist state to find that

capitalism is firmly entrenched and that big business is growing stronger at the expense of the little man. Tight credit
and high taxes make it virtually impossible for a newcomer
to get a start in business, whereas old, established industries
and concerns are earning greater profits than ever before and
turning the bulk of them into expansion. Taxation falls
heavily upon profits that are withdrawn, but is liberal when
it comes to reinvestment.

Big business is aggressively on the defensive against the inroads of the socialist state. As an illustration, the story is
told that former Finance Minister Per Edvin Sköld telephoned to Axelson Johnson, Sweden's leading shipping mag-
nate, and asked, "How much do you want for your merchant
fleet and how long can the Government have to pay for it?"

Johnson is said to have replied, "My ships aren't for sale,
but how much do you want for the railways? I'm ready to
pay cash."

Sweden is known for its iron ore, which goes into the manufacture of high-quality steel products at home and is largely
exported to steelmaking countries. Because of its strategic
value, it has played an important part in international relations, and the Swedes feared during the last world war that
it might provide a strong temptation to the Germans to invade their country. Geologists estimate that there is sufficient
iron ore to last for another two hundred years. Methods of
production are being kept abreast of the latest mechanical
developments, and mining executives are busy extending the
mines, increasing the ore capacity of the railways and en-
larging dock, shipping, and storage facilities. Last year's production of iron ore amounted to 14,000,000 tons, most of it
for export. Swedish iron ore is exported to West Germany,
Great Britain, the United States, Belgium, Luxemburg,
Poland, and Czechoslovakia, with the United States taking
about 12 per cent of the total.

The iron ore deposits are located in two areas: northern Lapland, where the richest mines are to be found; and the Bergslagen district in the central part of the country. One single company—Trafik Grängesberg-Oxelösund (known as TGO)—controls both mining areas and is accountable for 90 per cent of Sweden's total production of iron ore. The mines at Kiruna and Gällivare in Lapland are owned by the Luossavaara Kiruna Company (LKAB), in which the State now owns a half-interest, while the remainder of the shares are held by TGO. This partnership has been carried on, under pressure from the State, for close to half a century. It was a Conservative government which originally forced its way into the ore business, mainly to drive out foreign interests— British and German—and because it realized it would be good business. But when labor later came to power, it found a convenient precedent of which it has taken increasing advantage.

The State gained its foothold in the iron-ore business by controlling the railways which provide the sole outlet to the export harbors. Through this opening wedge, the Government gained its partnership in the mining, which yields it the lion's share of the business, and acquired the right to purchase the mines at ten-year intervals, the next of which is due on September 30, 1957. The Government has now given the company notice, with the approval of Parliament, that it intends to exercise that right next year unless the company is prepared to accept Government management. In either case, it means Government control of the mines and virtual nationalization of the iron-ore industry. This outcome has long been feared by big business, which feels that this example may be followed in other fields.

I have found considerable hesitation on the part of those most closely connected with the ore business to discuss past history. Evidently the executives of Grängesberg do not want to antagonize the Government, realizing that they have to make the best of an unwanted partnership; while Government spokesmen are reluctant to discuss a record of which they are none too proud. The background which follows has therefore been gathered most painstakingly, piecemeal, through interviews and from library sources, and is probably the only connected account of the complicated events which developed at the turn of the century.

Certainly the early beginnings are confusing. The existence of rich ore deposits in Lapland had been known for several centuries. Small prospectors staked out claims, and there were suits and countersuits. In the early part of the eighteenth century the Government sent a commission to investigate "two gigantic mountains of ore in the most desolate and inhospitable wilderness of the north." But the high phosphorus content of the ore was then considered to render the deposits almost worthless. These mountains are now the site of the two largest and most profitable Lapland mines.

TGO operates three mines in Lapland, north of the Arctic Circle. There is the Luossavaara mine at Kiruna, by far the largest, and there are the Malmberget (literally "ore mountain") and Koskullkulle mines at Gällivare. The output of these mines is carried by railway to the Norwegian port of Narvik, ice-free in winter, and to the Baltic port of Luleå. Narvik, which was bitterly fought over during the last world war and occupied by the Germans, has since been entirely rebuilt. The ore harbor at Luleå is peculiar; the level of the land is rising, so that the city had to move once and will have to move again someday. The ground was pressed down by the massive ice that lay over Scandinavia and retreated northward, and it now rises at the rate of three feet a century. The harbor is frozen six months of the year and closed to traffic; it is said that "hell is cold" in Luleå, where the temperature in the winter months sinks to 40 degrees below zero Fahrenheit and where there is only a couple of hours of daylight. Notwithstanding the rigorous climate, Luleå is a growing city and there are now 25,000 inhabitants in this Arctic outpost, all of them connected in some way with the ore business.

Another important ore mine is Grängesberg, from which the company derives its name, and is located in central Sweden and joined by rail to the Baltic ice-free port of Oxelösund. This mine and railway were the first in operation before the Thomas refining process was discovered in the late seventies, which made possible the use of phosphoric ores, previously regarded as of little value.

The British originally had a heavy stake in the exploitation of Swedish iron ore. It was a British company which obtained concessions in 1882 to exploit the Lapland ore deposits and to build the Arctic ore railway. According to the agreement, the railway was to be completed by 1891 and it was provided that the Swedish Government would have the right to purchase the line forty years after its completion. A British firm, the Swedish-Norwegian Railway Company Ltd., was established and the work of building the railway was given to Wilkinson and Jarvis, a London engineering concern.

By 1889 scarcely more than a third of the railway had been completed, the section extending from Luleå northward to Gällivare. When it was ready for official inspection, the Swedish Government found that it failed to meet the terms of the concession, since it was obviously impossible for the company to fulfill its promise of completing the entire line within another two years, particularly as the company was on the verge of bankruptcy. The Government then annulled the concession and took over the line, "purchasing" it from the British firm for 6,500,000 crowns ($1,300,000). Although the Government claimed that the company had failed to live up to its obligations, it was no secret that the main objective was to bring so important an enterprise for the country under State ownership and save it from foreign speculation. The Government itself undertook to complete the remainder of the line to the Swedish-Norwegian border. It was the Norwegian Government which built the short section joining the border with the port of Narvik. The line as a whole was completed in 1902.

It was when the State undertook to complete the ore railway after its purchase from the British that it forced its first agreement with the mining interests. In effect, it told them that if it was going to complete the railway, it wanted certain guarantees. An agreement was made setting a freight rate and a minimum amount of ore to be transported annually.

While the State was taking over the railway from the British, a group of Swedish businessmen was formed to acquire the mines from the hard-pressed British company. It was a double squeeze-play. This group was headed by Emil Gustaf Broms, Danish honorary consul at Nederkalix in Lapland, and included among others a Colonel C. O. Bergman who had earlier been associated with Broms in the lumber business in the far north. Bergman had some claims on the mines, and he brought suit against the British company, alleging that it had failed to maintain its rights by not regularly exploiting the mines. Bergman won his suit and together with Broms established the Gällivare Malmfält (iron ore) Company which first gained control of the Gällivare mines and later obtained a majority of the shares in the Luossavaara mine.

Broms was a hardy and ruthless pioneer, eager to amass a fortune. He was one of the main figures in the early development of the rich but merciless Arctic area of Sweden. He himself took an active part in the pioneering work. In the summer months he often tramped from his mines at Gällivare to Kiruna, a distance of some sixty miles through dense mosquito-infested forests, accompanied by his young wife. Aside from his mining interests, Broms owned a luxurious home in Stockholm, the present French Embassy, a country estate near the capital, and he was one of the principal backers of *Svenska Dagbladet,* the leading conservative newspaper. He also purchased a large farm tract in the far north where old mineworkers could retire and own their homes. As a hobby, he financed scientific expeditions to Spitzbergen and Greenland.

But Broms and his companions soon ran into trouble. They had received large bank loans to finance their mining operations and were unable to repay them. They offered the mines for sale to a German syndicate and were about to conclude an agreement with the Nord Deutsches Bank in Hamburg when TGO stepped in at the last moment and purchased them. TGO appealed to the Swedish Government for a loan of $4,000,000 to help in the purchase, but this was turned down by Parliament, which regarded the venture as hazardous. The deal was nonetheless consummated with the help of other German capital. Thus, while the front door was closed to one German group, the back door was opened to another, although it did not obtain a controlling interest. TGO paid $1,780,000 for the mines, but it also undertook to pay off the debts of Broms and his partners, which amounted to as much as $9,200,000. On his own behalf Broms made a characteristically shrewd deal. He obtained a royalty of two cents for every ton of ore mined up to a million tons a year and one cent for every ton in excess of that amount, to be paid to him and his descendants for a period of fifty years. Broms died soon after the agreement was signed in 1903, but his heirs continued to collect the royalty until two years ago.

TGO had earlier received support from the British financier Sir Ernest Cassel. It was in the eighties that the legendary figure of the financial wizard and adviser to King Edward VII first entered the picture. Cassel was the son of a small Jewish banker from Cologne. At an early age he emigrated to England and became a naturalized subject on the day of his marriage to the daughter of a British banker. Three years later he became a Catholic by her dying wish. Cassel first met King Edward at the races, and a close friendship developed between the two men which eventually led Cassel to become a privy councilor and the closest adviser to the spendthrift monarch on financial matters.

Cassel's interest in Sweden was first focused on the Grängesberg ore mine, but as his ventures prospered, he widened his activities. It was Cassel who first realized the importance of the Thomas process for the conversion of phosphoric ores, which revolutionized the Swedish ore business and also enabled the Germans to make their rapid advance in the steel business, outdistancing the British. Cassel took part in financing the building of the ore railway from Grängesberg to Oxelösund, which flourished once the phosphoric ores became valuable, and later acquired a large share in the Lapland mines. It was Cassel's Swedish investments that contributed to the fortune of $35,000,000 which he left upon his death in 1921. Cassel's granddaughter, Edwina Ashley, is now the wife of Lord Louis Mountbatten, brother of the present Queen of Sweden.

The negotiations for the purchase of the Lapland mines by TGO and their amalgamation with the Grängesberg mine were brought to their successful conclusion through the efforts of Arvid Lindman, one-time director of the Luossavaara mine, who later, as Prime Minister of a Conservative government in 1907, forced TGO into an agreement whereby the State renounced its threat to tax the export of iron ore and, in return, gained a half-interest in the Lapland mines and the right to purchase them at ten-year intervals. In 1927, the Government made a new agreement with the mines which remains in effect, with only slight changes, up to the present. Under this agreement, the profits are distributed equally up to 3,750,000 tons of ore mined, while any amount in excess is divided on a basis of two-thirds to the State and one-third to the company. Inasmuch as the output of the Lapland mines now approximates 12,000,000 tons a year, the State receives the largest share of the profit.

The price for the Government's purchase of the mines was fixed in these agreements at twenty-five times half of the average annual profit over the preceding ten-year period. If the Government now purchases the mines, it will have to pay $195,000,000 in ten annual installments. The payments are to be tax-free, but the Government will recover some of the amount from tax returns of individual beneficiaries.

LKAB is still considered a private concern, notwithstanding the Government's participation and influence. The company is administered by a board of directors, four appointed by the company—including the chairman of the board and the managing director—and four by the State. Since the managing director is entitled to cast the deciding vote, the management is actually in private hands, although there has been need, of course, for close co-operation with the State.

The present managing director of both TGO and LKAB is Erland Waldenstrom, a forty-four-year-old chemical engineer who spent most of his business life in the timber industry and was the chief engineer of one of the largest pulp mills until he was appointed to succeed his father in his present post five years ago.

There is something of the atmosphere of the house of Morgan about Waldenstrom personally and the head offices of TGO in Stockholm. There is the same austerity and aversion to publicity which has characterized the great Wall Street banking firm. Waldenstrom is tall, suave, reticent, aloof, and there is a coolness about his manner that might well be associated with the frozen north where his mines are located. The offices of TGO are pompous and there is a clash of modernism and of the old. The managing director sits at his desk, clear of papers, with a loudspeaking device at his elbow for inter-office communication, and converses at length over the telephone with London, Paris, and other world capitals as if he were making local calls. The furniture is heavy, stiff, and formal. There is an alabaster chandelier in the center of the room and the walls are covered with paintings of snow scenes—the ore mountains.

Waldenstrom speaks perfect English in a low-modulated voice. He says he knows little of the company's history and referred me to the library of Parliament for information, remarking that a great deal was said about it in 1927 when the basic agreement was made with the Government. He estimates that at least 90 per cent of the company's profit goes to the State. First, he relates, 50 per cent is spent for State and municipal taxes, then 60 per cent of what is left goes to the State for its share of the business, and over 50 per cent of the remainder is paid by individual shareholders in income tax. Actually the shareholders, many of them wealthy industrialists, have paid an average of 70 per cent in taxes on their shares. Waldenstrom's salary for operating a business with a turnover of $100,000,000 a year is listed in the official tax calendar at $34,000, but this does not take into account the profit from his own holdings.

The company's profits increased steadily until the peak year 1953, when TGO reported a profit of $13,278,000 and LKAB, of $49,445,000. This dropped off in 1954 to $12,240,-000 for TGO and $39,023,000 for LKAB. The decline was due to the general recession in the iron and steel industries in western Europe and the United States following the end of the Korean War. Only half of these profits have been distributed to shareholders; the remainder has been set aside for further development. The point has been reached where the ore veins above surface are nearly exhausted and a shift must be made to underground mining. This requires new machinery and new capital investment.

In addition to operating the mines, the company has built the dock installations at the ore ports and has its own fleet of twenty modern tankers which carry ore on their outward journey and bring back oil. These vessels vary in size from 3,000 tons to 25,000 tons. The ore railway has turned into a most profitable enterprise for the State, earning close to $20,-000,000 a year on the line, making up the entire deficit which the State railways would otherwise incur on their over-all traffic.

The Government's decision to take over the ore mines came unexpectedly in March, 1955. No one had believed that the Government would pay such a vast sum as $195,000,000 to acquire the remaining 10 per cent of the profit of the mines that still goes into private hands. Furthermore, the operation of the mines has been among the most progressive and efficient of any Swedish enterprise and the 3,000 mineworkers have been as well cared for as any industrial group. Such a large expenditure also threatens to increase inflation, which the Government is committed to combat.

In the debate in Parliament, former Finance Minister Sköld said it was to be now or never. What he apparently meant was that the Government had better act now rather than wait for the end of another ten-year period when the profits would be still greater and the cost of purchase that much higher. The Government failed to take advantage of its option in 1947 when the mines could have been bought for half of the present price. Mr. Sköld's explanation, however, was that he was concerned for the future of the mineworkers in case of hard times and that only the State could guarantee their welfare. Professor Bertil Ohlin, leader of the Liberal opposition party, pointed out that the company had a reserve fund of $50,000,000, which should be sufficient to cope with any business recession. But this was a side issue, since the Government was entitled to exercise its prerogative of purchasing the mines and was determined to do so.

The State also has a stake in the forests, which cover over half of Sweden's territory and play a vital role in the country's economy. Timber and wood products account for the largest part of exports, and while Sweden has lost some of the American pulp market in recent years, she still retains a dominant position as a supplier to western European countries.

The Government, municipalities, and the churches together own a quarter of the forest land, while big business firms own an equal amount and the remainder is in the hands of private individuals, mostly farmers. Virtually every Swedish farmer, whatever the size of his farm, owns some woodland as an extra source of income and fells the trees during the winter months and delivers them to the co-operative Forestry Association, which pays him the standard price and markets the timber for him.

A century ago, Swedish mills concentrated on the production of sawn and planed lumber, but increased processing methods have led to the development of a variety of other wood products, particularly chemical pulp—now the largest export—newsprint, wrapping paper, wallboard, prefabricated houses, and many other items. But Sweden's timber production, unlike the seemingly inexhaustible supply of iron ore, has its limitations. The virgin forests have been overcut and the output is now limited to the annual growth. In the north, where there are vast forest tracts, the rate of growth is slow and it takes 120 years for a tree to reach maturity for sawn lumber and seventy years for pulp. In central and southern Sweden, however, the rate of growth is quicker; forests are denser and produce five times as much timber per acre, but the quality is inferior. Forestry officials hope that the production from the southern areas will counterbalance the decline in the north, which is due to continue for the next fifty years.

Transportation of timber from the forests to the mills is constantly being improved. In the north, the logs are floated down the numerous rivers and streams to the coast, where the principal mills are located. This intricate water network, over double the mileage of the railroads, is so extensive that the distance to the water from the locality where any tree is felled is scarcely ever more than a couple of miles, covered by horse sleigh or tractor. In the southern part of the country the transportation is by truck and railroad, which is far more expensive.

Two Government agencies represent the State's interest in forestry and function under the Ministry of Agriculture. They are the Board of Crown Lands and Forests and the Board of Forestry. The former administers the Government's 10,000,000 acres of forestland and operates some sawmills and pulp factories in the north which were started in times of depression to relieve unemployment; however, the Government sells most of its timber to private manufacturers. The Board of Forestry exercises supervision over all remaining forest land which is under private ownership, with particular emphasis on conservation. It makes sure that only a certain amount of timber is cut, so as to preserve the forests for the future, but it allows private companies some leeway in order to take advantage of favorable markets. It helps in the planting of new areas, subsidizes road-building, and educates officials in forestry methods. It is, in fact, the policy-making board. Wilhelm Plym-Forshell, Director-General of the Board of Forestry, points out that inasmuch as forestry provides a livelihood for more than a million persons in Sweden, the State cannot be indifferent to private management and that restrictions are therefore unavoidable.

The fluctuations in the export of chemical pulp in recent years have been marked by precipitous rises and falls, varying between an export total of 60,000 to 300,000 tons a month. The peak was reached in the summer of 1951, but the bottom suddenly dropped out of the market when the United States imposed a ceiling on pulp prices. Exports which sank to half have now recovered to about 200,000 tons a month, while the average price has fallen from $350 a ton to $125. The profit of the big companies was so great during the boom that the Swedish Government found it necessary to drain it off to prevent inflation by imposing what it called an "equalization fee" on exports, actually a tax, a part of which was to be refunded to the companies over a period of years while the remainder was set aside for welfare projects for forestry workers. Inasmuch as new and expanded American and Canadian mills have entered into the pulp business since the Korean War, Swedish exporters will probably never recover the American market as it existed before.

The biggest of the Swedish private companies is Cellulosa, which is located in and about the lumber town of Sundsvall in northern Sweden. It sells over $100,000,000 of wood products annually, most of them exported. It is responsible for close to a quarter of the entire output of private timber firms. Its products are exported to western Europe, the United States, South America, Australia, and Indonesia.

An item in one of Cellulosa's reports disclosed recently that a railway is being built from one of the company's mills at Munksund to the Baltic port of Pitea as part of the Government's program for unemployment relief. Obviously, the directors of the timber company are well aware of the methods used by the Government in its invasion of the iron-ore business by means of the railways. The new railway is being financed to the extent of 80 per cent by public funds, including 60 per cent from the Government's unemployment board and 20 per cent from the local municipality, with the company putting up the remaining 20 per cent. The railway is a short line, only six miles from the mill to the sea, but it may give the Government its first foothold in the private timber industry.

Arguments for nationalization of the timber industry have been put forward at intervals and were advanced again recently at a meeting of the Social Democratic Youth Association. It was charged that the private companies made inordinate profits when times were good and that in the event of a depression, the Government would have to bear the burden of unemployment. The association claimed that the violent fluctuations in the timber market, particularly pulp, within recent years could have been avoided by Government control of the industry. The Government, it was said, would also be in a better position to deal with unemployment by shifting labor. The association was careful, however, to exclude individual forest owners from the scope of nationalization, since it realized that many of them are small farmers and some of them party members.

In rebuttal, Axel Enström, managing director of Cellulosa, declared that it is beyond Sweden's power to control the fluctuations in the international market, whether the timber industry is in private or Government hands, and that forestry workers are just as well looked after by private enterprise as they would be by the State.

There is no reason to believe that the Swedish Government contemplates nationalization of the timber industry in the near future, but it is holding this possibility in reserve, and in the event of a depression, it seems certain that it would become a live issue.

Swedish industry depends to a large extent on water power, which is so highly developed that Sweden ranks third in the world in electrical output per capita after Canada and Norway and on a par with the United States. The electrification in towns and villages is complete, and only homes in remote localities in the northern mountain and forest area are without electricity because the cost of the lines would be prohibitive. All the principal railway lines have been electrified.

The output of power last year reached twenty billion kilowatt-hours, a third of the estimated water power available in the country if all the rivers were harnessed to capacity. The State Power Administration has plans to increase the output by half within the next five years, and it is estimated that if the present increasing demand for consumption is maintained, it will be possible to make full use of Sweden's water-power resources by 1980. This would greatly reduce the need for fuels such as coal, which Sweden is now compelled to import from Poland, Britain, the United States, and the Ruhr. The Swedes are especially anxious to rid themselves of dependence on Polish coal, for which they have to enter into hard-fought barter negotiations annually with the Soviet satellite state.

There are some 1,400 power plants in Sweden, including a score of large ones. One of the first and largest was built early in the century at Trollhättan, north of Gothenburg and close to Sweden's biggest lake, Vänern, which serves as a reservoir. This plant, however, long ago proved inadequate for the needs of the country, and both the Government and private enterprise have since turned their attention to the rivers and rapids of the north. Porjus on the Lule River, above the

Arctic Circle, was built by the State mainly to supply power to the ore railways and the mines; and in 1953 another great plant, Harsprånget (literally Hare's Leap), was completed farther south along the same river, establishing two records. It is the largest power plant in western Europe, with units only second in size to the gigantic American Grand Coulee station, and the power is transmitted at 380,000 volts over the highest tension power line in the world, exceeding the 287,000-volt transmission line between Hoover Dam and Los Angeles. This power line now runs to Hallsberg in southern Sweden, a distance of 600 miles, but is being extended to the port city of Gothenburg and to the southern tip of Sweden, thus carrying light generated in the land of the midnight sun the full length of the country. The extremely high voltage makes it possible to transmit the power over a single cable instead of the four power lines that would otherwise be needed if Sweden had continued the 220,000 volts used previously. It also makes transmission possible with the least possible loss of power. The station at Harsprånget produces 350,000 kilowatts and was built at a cost of $52,000,000.

Another record was established in 1953 when a direct-current cable was laid from the Swedish mainland to the island of Gottland in the Baltic, an important military base. It is the largest cable of its kind and was made necessary by the fact that Gottland has no water power of its own.

The new power stations in Sweden are built in solid granite rock, characteristic of the country, far underground. This is, above all, a security measure in case of war, and the same technique of bore-hole drilling is employed as in the construction of the several hundred underground air and naval stations and shelters located throughout the country. The plant at Harsprånget, for instance, goes down 250 feet below surface, and the underground space may be compared to a five-story building.

Construction of a series of new power stations is underway and will be completed within the next three years, including a larger plant than any yet built at Stornorrfors on the Ume River, south of the Lule River, with a capacity of 375,000 kilowatts. All these plants will eventually be joined with the new network of high-tension lines which is linked with Norway and Denmark.

There is close co-operation between the Government and private enterprise in the development of water power, a co-operation born of necessity during the last world war when Sweden was critically short of fuel, particularly coal, and became increasingly dependent upon power. This co-operation is being continued, and the State and private enterprise each spend as much as $250,000 every working day in new development of water power. The Government is responsible for 40 per cent of production; the municipalities, 6 per cent; and private enterprise is accountable for the remainder. Industry takes a third for its own use, but the main power lines have been built by the State. Distribution of electrical power is in the hands of the municipalities and local co-operative organizations.

To supplement Sweden's water power, Åke Rusch, director of the State Power Administration, has revealed plans to build four or five reactors within the next eight years to generate both heat and electricity, placing Sweden in the forefront among the nations of the world in the development of atomic power for peaceful purposes. The first reactor, to be known as "Adam," will be located in the industrial city of Vasteras and will produce heating for its 68,000 inhabitants, while the second one, to be called "Eve," will be built in southern Sweden to provide electricity. Rusch declared: "We are fortunate in having the time to develop our atomic power before our water-power resources are fully tapped."

Premier Erlander has also disclosed that Sweden may have

the largest supply of uranium in Europe, an amount sufficient to meet the country's own needs for several thousand years. He told Parliament that there are four and a half billion tons of shale in the provinces of Närke, in central Sweden, and Västergötland, in the southern part of the country, and that if only a third of this is exploited, it would mean a supply of 150,000 tons of uranium. The trouble is that the cost of extracting uranium from the shale—by a secret Swedish process—is more than the price of uranium on the world market; but if it can be reduced, as it no doubt will in time, Sweden may well become one of the principal suppliers of this valuable product. Sweden's uranium supply recalls the early experience with the iron ore before the Thomas refining process was discovered.

Notwithstanding the Government's participation in the main sources of production, over three-quarters of the nation's business remains in the hands of private enterprise. Swedish businessmen have learned to take advantage of all the loopholes which the Government has left them both in the conduct of their business and in taxation. They are alert, enterprising, up-to-date, and they realize the importance of mechanization and of keeping abreast of the latest industrial developments in a country where there is a chronic shortage of labor in prosperous times. This is a factor which makes Swedish businessmen conscious of the need for treating labor with special consideration, irrespective of public-welfare projects. The emphasis in industry is on efficiency, increased production, and on co-operation to the extent that it can be carried on without sacrificing competition.

Some businessmen and industrial leaders are obviously nervous about the future and what they may expect if labor continues in power. But few leaders, either in business or government, believe that there will be any radical change in the business structure. Even the Social Democratic politician

Richard Sterner, one of the most outspoken advocates of further socialization, believes that private industry will continue to be the backbone of the nation. "Further development toward democracy," Sterner says, "will take place mainly without change of ownership of the means of production. That part of the economy which is controlled by the State and the municipalities will, of course, be broadened, but such changes will occur only gradually when they are called for by practical necessity, and in no case will they have a revolutionary character. As far as we can see into the future, private and co-operative enterprise will dominate the Swedish economy."

CHAPTER III

Consumers' Co-operatives

ALTHOUGH Sweden was not a pioneer in the co-operative movement, it provides the outstanding example of what the co-operatives can accomplish, and the movement is gaining steadily in influence and is playing an ever-increasing role in the Swedish economy. Actually, Sweden was the third Scandinavian country to turn to the co-operative movement, following Denmark and Norway, and was only ahead of Finland.

The Swedish co-operative movement dates back a century, but it is debatable whether its start was a spontaneous one within the country or whether it derived its inspiration from the British Rochdale movement. Whatever the case, the Rochdale co-operatives set a pattern for the Swedish movement and certainly influenced it later.

The first co-operative society in Sweden was founded in 1851 with the support of Robert von Kraemer, Governor of Uppsala province. Von Kraemer was an intimate friend of Erik Gustaf Geijer, famous Swedish poet and historian who had studied the Rochdale co-operatives and enthusiastically described the British venture. This is the only link between the British experiment and the Swedish one at the time of its inception.

The first Swedish co-operative was established by farmers in the small town of Örsundsbro. The farmers had a surplus of grain, and they bartered it for tar, bricks, paint, nails, salt, iron, and herring, which they retailed through their co-operative. It is not generally known that this initial experiment, which was regarded as a daring socialistic step in those days, was made possible by the personal intervention of the reformist King Oscar I. It was necessary for the new society to obtain a license to operate a store, and it was discussed by the cabinet, which was divided on the issue. The King prevailed over his cabinet, and thus the first co-operative was started with royal support.

It is no less interesting to note that one of the first co-operatives established in Stockholm two decades later included among its members King Charles XV and several of his courtiers. The last member of the royal family to support the co-operative movement was the late Prince Eugen, brother of the late King Gustav V. No members of the present royal family are associated with the co-operatives.

The Örsundsbro experiment survived only a decade. A second experiment at the Kloster Iron Works in the province of Dalecarlia, a few years later, was more fortunate and has continued to this day. It was established by the ironworkers to supply their own needs, and it pursued such an independent course that it still remains outside the orbit of *Kooperativa Förbundet* (Co-operative Union and Wholesale Society), popularly known as KF, which is the central organ of the Swedish co-operative movement.

In the 1880's a so-called ring movement got under way among progressive labor elements to secure rebates for members from private traders. But these early co-operative efforts had little success at a time when Sweden was experiencing a severe rural depression which led 350,000 Swedes to emigrate to the United States within the space of a decade. It was only when Sweden turned from agriculture to industrial development at the close of the century and emerged from the depression that the co-operative movement gained a foothold. Some forty co-operative societies joined at a congress in Stockholm in 1899 to establish KF, which gave the first real impetus to the movement. It was originally intended that KF should be only a connecting link between the local consumer societies, but within a few years it was acting as buyer and supplier for them. Since then KF has entered into production and has become the directing force in the movement.

The establishment of KF was brought about mainly through the efforts of two men from widely separated walks of life: the liberal G. H. von Koch, son of an army officer, and Axel Rylander, a socialist labor leader and political agitator. It was obviously not easy for these men, although they shared the same ambition, to merge their views. Von Koch stood for social reform, but he wanted the co-operatives to keep clear of politics; Rylander envisaged the co-operative movement as an instrument of labor and wanted to link it to the Social Democratic Party, of which he was secretary. From the outset, more than half of KF's supporters were Social Democrats, gathered from the labor ranks; but the movement has kept outside of politics to the extent that it has not been openly identified with any party and that membership is open to all, regardless of party affiliation. The relationship between the co-operative movement and the Social Democratic Party has been described to me by Professor Gunnar Silverstolpe, one of the foremost authorities on the Swedish co-operative movement, as a "moral alliance."

The difference in viewpoints which separated von Koch and Rylander fifty years ago still persists. Professor Silverstolpe says the co-operative movement has a split personality:

there are two forces within the movement. One, following von Koch's views, is liberal (middle-of-the-road in Swedish political terms); the other is linked with the trade unions and the labor movement. Albin Johansson, Chairman of the board of directors of KF and the leading spirit in the co-operative movement, is on the liberal side, while Mauritz Bonow, Secretary General of KF and frequently mentioned as a possible successor to the aging Johansson, is more closely connected with the labor movement.

The idea of establishing a central organization originated with von Koch upon his return from a visit to England, where he studied the Rochdale co-operatives. It took great courage for von Koch, a member of the Swedish aristocracy, to champion what was then regarded as an advanced socialistic experiment; and he was equally unpopular with the upper classes and with the workers, who at first distrusted him. He became the first secretary of KF, but he was not the fighter the movement needed in those early days, and he soon relinquished the task to Martin Sundell, a linotype operator whose almost fanatical devotion to the co-operative cause sparked its spectacular rise. It was typical of the co-operative movement that the three pioneers—von Koch, Rylander, and Sundell—were all connected with the temperance movement which exerted so much influence in Sweden at the turn of the century.

Sundell came from a poor family. His father was a carpenter and died young, leaving his widow with five children to raise. They necessarily grew up in poverty, but Mrs. Sundell proudly boasted that she never had to ask for a cent from anyone. It was this fighting spirit that young Martin inherited and brought to the co-operative movement.

Sundell became interested in the co-operatives after hearing one of von Koch's speeches, and took a leading part in the establishment of a local co-operative society and store in his native town of Köping, where he was employed in a printing plant. He made his first contact with KF when he came to Stockholm, at the age of twenty-four, as a representative of the Köping society at a co-operative congress. Two years later he succeeded von Koch as secretary of KF and as editor of *Kooperatören* (*The Co-operator*), the biweekly co-operative journal.

From then on Sundell devoted himself wholeheartedly to the co-operative movement. He saw it as an instrument for promoting the welfare of the workers by providing them with the necessities of life at lower cost and thereby raising their standard of living; he also believed that the co-operative movement, if it became international, would be a strong force for peace in the world.

Typical of his faith, Sundell used to say that the co-operative movement "will become great the day we want it to." He preached two fundamental principles: all co-operative business should be on a cash basis; and the co-operatives should set aside a reserve fund to build up capital needed for expansion. In other words, the movement was to pay its own way and stand on its own feet. Furthermore, Sundell wanted the co-operatives to keep out of politics. "It may be difficult," he remarked characteristically, "but difficult does not mean impossible."

The fighting linotype operator died of tuberculosis at the age of thirty-one, but in the short space of a decade he brought to the co-operative movement the dynamic leadership which was needed to give it a real start and bequeathed to it that aggressive spirit that continues to carry it forward to new high levels with each passing year. In his obituaries, he was referred to as "the fiery soul that burned out."

The co-operative movement has grown steadily over the past fifty years, and it is remarkable that there has been no setback at any time during this period, even during depression. The figures are impressive. When Sundell died, there were 75,000 members, while at the start of 1955 there were 1,070,000 members, most of them representing families. Since the average Swedish family consists of 3.5 members, approximately half of Sweden's population belongs to co-operatives. This in itself indicates the tremendous influence of the movement within the country.

The growth of the movement is due, in large part, to the easy manner in which membership is acquired. It is a rule that a member must own shares to the value of 150 Swedish crowns ($30), but he need not put up the cash. Anyone can buy in a co-operative store, whether a member of a co-operative society or not, and can accumulate the necessary amount to purchase the shares from dividends over a period of time. The dividends usually amount to 3 per cent. Once the shares have been paid up, the customer becomes a full-fledged member and is entitled to receive his dividends on all purchases from the co-operative store as well as an interest of about 4 per cent on his shares. This means that anyone can afford to join a co-operative.

A set of fairly simple rules govern the co-operatives and must be accepted by the local societies which are members of KF. Sundell's principle that all business must be on a cash basis still stands, but is no longer so rigidly enforced. Co-operative leaders, and foremost among them Albin Johansson, claim that by tightening credit, the co-operatives have removed a burden of debt from the shoulders of a large section of the Swedish people and strengthened their integrity. The people, they argue, are less tempted to buy beyond their means than if installment buying were a regular practice, and are better masters of their own economy.

Other rules provide that all are eligible to co-operative membership; that each member is entitled to one vote in his local society; that each year, as Sundell advocated, the profits of a co-operative store in excess of a small fixed percentage shall be set aside for expansion. No *konsum* store can obtain more than thirty days' credit for its purchases from KF. This is sometimes stretched to enable new stores to get a start, but that is the only exception.

There are now 688 local co-operative societies in Sweden connected with KF, and they operate 8,077 stores throughout the country. The total retail turnover in 1954 amounted to $488,000,000. KF's turnover as a producer whose products are also marketed outside of the co-operatives amounted to $160,-000,000.

The size of the local co-operatives varies from the Stockholm *Konsum*, the largest in the country, which operates 879 stores, has a membership of 160,000, and does a business of over $90,000,000 annually, to the small village co-operative society with a membership of less than a hundred. The *cooperativa* or *konsum*—as the local stores are called—is as much of a landmark in a Swedish village as the church, the school, the community center, the bank, or the movie.

The local co-operative stores may well be compared with the American chain grocery stores. They deal mainly in foodstuffs and account for over 20 per cent of the national turnover. They handle groceries, meat, bread, milk, vegetables, and an assortment of household goods, many of them produced in KF factories. The stores are usually among the most modern buildings in the towns and villages, and many of them are designed by KF architects, with an eye on efficiency first. They are scrupulously clean, and their windows are neatly arranged by specialists trained in KF display methods. The service in many co-operative stores excels that in private stores. Ample personnel is maintained as a matter of policy, and extra help is hired on weekends and rush days. Whatever opinion Swedes may hold about the co-operatives, and this is a controversial subject, they are agreed that they have raised the standard of grocery stores throughout the country by their example.

In rural areas, the small co-operative stores specialize in goods for the farmers, and in some cases their turnover is surprisingly large. I visited a small co-operative store in Forssa, an agricultural suburb of Katrineholm, which had an annual turnover of $40,000. It dealt in a wide variety of commodities—plows, shovels, rakes, acetylene lamps, horseshoes, grain, and fertilizer—intended to meet the needs of the local farmers who came from miles around. The profit, according to the store's manager, was 4 per cent, of which 3 per cent was refunded as dividends to customers at the year's end, while 1 per cent was set aside for expansion of business.

The co-operatives make a particular effort to serve scattered rural communities where no stores exist. Local co-operative societies operate buses equipped as stores on regular scheduled routes in isolated areas. Customers know when to expect the bus and can place advance orders. This service accounts for a large share of the rural business.

The relationship between the local co-operative societies and KF is a loose one and affords the societies considerable leeway and independence. They may buy as much as they want from KF and obtain the advantages of low prices and easy delivery, but they are free to purchase elsewhere. In 1954, the local co-operative societies bought 35 per cent of their stock from KF. The Stockholm *Konsum* purchased only 20 per cent of its goods from KF, whereas co-operative stores in small towns and remote areas purchased close to 50 per cent. This is due to the fact that the larger societies produce some of their own goods and can more easily obtain other products. Stockholm *Konsum,* for instance, has its own bakery and mineral-water plant.

The largest co-operative store in Sweden is a department store in Stockholm operated by KF, known as PUB, the initials of its former owner Paul U. Bergström, who sold out to the co-operatives twenty years ago. PUB deals in medium-quality goods at low but by no means bargain prices. It is well above the level of Sweden's five-and-ten chain stores (known as *Tempo* and *Epa*), but falls short of the standard of the fashionable *Nordiska Kompaniet,* Stockholm's leading department store patronized by the royal family and the elite.

For the most part PUB carries goods produced by co-operative factories, but it also sells other standard wares at the regular prices. It specializes in ready-made clothing and particularly in a wide variety of women's wear. Wedding gowns are priced from as little as $35 to $60 in white satin with appropriate frills. Modern furniture is cheap, and velvety finished mahogany veneer tables and desks sell for only $30. But household goods are expensive in comparison with the American equivalent. Sets of fifty pieces of chinaware run between $80 and $100 for a quality similar to that in the American Woolworth stores.

It is in the industrial field that KF has achieved its greatest success. KF owns seventy-one factories, has at least a half-interest in fourteen others, and a part ownership in another thirty-eight. Some of these factories are among the largest in Sweden, and their efficiency is on a par with the best Swedish industries. KF's enterprises produce such commodities as margarine, vegetable oils, flour, cereals, bread, canned goods, chocolate, meat products, fertilizers, farm implements, rubber goods including galoshes and tires, electric light bulbs, staple fiber, insulating material, wallboard, scales, charcoal, chemicals, furniture, pottery, cash registers, and many other goods designed principally for the Swedish consumer, some of which are also exported. The co-operative congresses have not clearly established the scope of KF's industrial activities but, in principle, the policy has been to lay stress on the production of consumer goods rather than raw materials. KF officials declare frankly, however, that there is no limit to the industrial fields which KF may enter.

It was Albin Johansson who, when he succeeded Sundell as Secretary of KF in 1910, launched the Swedish co-operatives into industry. Johansson became impressed, on a visit to Germany, with the importance of industry in the co-operative movement. This opened up an entirely new field for the Swedish co-operatives, with almost unlimited possibilities. But Johansson had to reckon, in the first place, with strong opposition from many of the local societies, which considered that the co-operatives should limit themselves to foodstuffs. It required an intensive campaign to convince them of the wisdom of branching out into other lines. This proved to be a turning point in the Swedish co-operative movement.

KF opened its battle against the monopolies with its attack on the margarine cartel forty years ago. It first instigated a boycott of the products of the two largest factories belonging to the cartel. When this was not completely successful, KF purchased a small factory and later built a larger one. As a result, the price of margarine was cut by 60 per cent, resulting in a saving of $2,000,000 annually to the Swedish consumers. At the same time, the demand for margarine increased to such an extent that Swedish production was quadrupled and the labor employed was doubled. Executives of the Swedish co-operatives contend that their price-cutting policy thus actually benefits business.

KF's successful attack on the margarine trust encouraged it to wage the battle successively against other cartels. The next fight was against the flour millers. In 1922, KF acquired the Three Crowns, one of the biggest flour mills, located at the entrance to Stockholm Bay and, two years later, the Three Lions mill in Gothenburg. With these two mills in its possession, KF was able to control the market and cut the price.

KF now produces approximately one-fifth of the flour consumed in Sweden.

In the same way, KF broke a number of other big cartels,
forcing price reductions in galoshes, tires, electric light bulbs,
superphosphates, fertilizers, pottery, and building materials.
KF found in all cases that it was able to break the price level
by controlling between 15 and 25 per cent of the output of
the product. KF executives emphasize that they do not aim
to establish a monopoly of their own in any field or to eliminate private competition, but that they only seek to obtain
a sufficient foothold to force prices down for the benefit of
the consumer.

Totally or partially owned KF industries are capitalized
at $40,000,000. The largest of these is the vegetable-oil fac-
tory at Karlshamn, which is capitalized at $6,000,000. It was
established originally to provide raw materials for the margarine factory and to make it independent of imports, especially in critical times. During World War II this oil factory
played an important part in providing the country with
scarce fats.

One of KF's most spectacular fights was directed against
the International Light Bulb Cartel, with headquarters in
Geneva. The outcome was KF's construction of its own electric light bulb factory, known as Luma, erected in 1931 in
the outskirts of Stockholm. The Luma factory, which was
started with a staff of seventy-five workers, now employs 1,500
workers and turns out 15,000,000 lamps a year. In the twenty-
five years of its existence, it has supplied over 100,000,000
bulbs.

Luma's entry into the field forced down the price of electric light bulbs in Sweden by 40 per cent. Luma only makes
the filament for the lamps and fits the glass globe over it,
but plans are now underway for the construction of a new
factory which will produce the outer globe and may bring

about a further price cut. Officials of Luma are proud to point out that although the cost of raw materials and labor has risen 100 per cent over the past twenty years, Luma has only increased the price of a 25-watt lamp by one cent. This has been made possible, Luma officials explain, by greater efficiency and increased production.

The Swedish Luma factory is linked with the Norwegian and British co-operative movements. There is a Luma plant in Oslo, Norway, and one in Glasgow, Scotland. The Stockholm factory supplies 38 per cent of the Swedish home market, which it shares with five other private companies: Osram, formerly owned by the co-operatives but returned to private enterprise, Tungsram, Skandia, Birka, and Vasa. Of Luma's production, 30 per cent goes to Swedish co-operative stores, which are the only ones allowed to retail the Luma lamps; 40 per cent to Swedish government offices; while the remaining 30 per cent is exported principally to Latin-American countries.

The distribution of Luma's output confronts KF with a delicate problem. It is impossible for KF to pay a dividend to the Government on its purchases of lamps since dividends are only paid to co-operative members, and the same holds true with regard to exports. This means that no dividend is paid on 70 per cent of Luma's output, which is set aside instead for expansion of the business. This is in conflict with the co-operative policy of profit-sharing and is a source of grave embarrassment to KF officials.

Although the Luma factory is twenty-five years old, it is one of the best in Europe. There are no doubt gaps in the assembly line which could be filled with more modern machinery, but the factory is operated with the same efficiency characteristic of KF headquarters. There is a free relationship between employer and employee which permits workers to take complaints directly to factory executives.

While co-operative factories are generally devoted to the manufacture of utilitarian goods, the Gustavsberg porcelain factory is an exception, and produces art work, too. The factory dates back to the seventeenth century and was purchased by KF in 1937 and modernized. It is now one of the largest in Sweden, on a par with Rörstrand, and employs 1,400 workers. It produces low-cost tableware and pottery works of art as well as bathroom fixtures and bathtubs.

KF's wage scale is identical with that of private industry, and expert knowledge or talent is highly paid. Thus Hjalmar Olson, director of the Gustavsberg factory, receives a salary three times that of Albin Johansson, Chairman of the board of KF. The same holds true for the well-known trio of artists, William Kage, Stig Lindberg, and Berndt Friberg, whose decorative porcelain and pottery, largely inspired by Chinese art, are familiar throughout Sweden.

The only enterprise owned by KF and ever returned to private ownership was the Osram Electric Works, manufacturers of electric light bulbs. This factory was a subsidiary of a German company in which the American General Electric owned a 20 per cent interest. After World War II it was taken over by the Swedish Government and sold to satisfy Swedish claims against Germany arising out of the war. There were two bids for Osram. A Swedish consortium, consisting of a group of private businessmen and some former employees of Osram, entered a bid, but KF topped it by $25,000 and acquired Osram for $2,140,000. Four months later KF sold the factory to the consortium without ever having operated it.

Various reasons are advanced for KF's abandoning Osram. There was some opposition on the part of the workers, who objected to being taken over by the co-operatives, but this was not a deciding factor. It involved a matter of co-operative principle. Osram lamps had been widely sold in private stores in Sweden, but if KF policy were adhered to, they could only be sold in co-operative stores in competition with KF's own Luma lamps. This would have meant that a large part of Osram's trade would have been lost to some other brand of lamp manufactured by private business. It is also said that the private stores were unwilling to handle Osram lamps even if KF had been prepared to sell them outside of the co-operatives.

KF sold Osram to the consortium for what it had paid for the factory. There was no financial loss involved, but KF executives recall this experience with some bitterness. It is KF's only business failure in half a century of co-operative enterprise.

CHAPTER IV

The Big Seven

WHILE Sweden's co-operative enterprise is run by a complicated series of committees and boards, the leadership of the movement is actually in the hands of seven top directors. They are the real bosses of the co-operative movement. They direct its business, determine its growth, and plan its future. They themselves would deny it. They would say that the movement springs from the people and rests with the common man in city, town, or country. They would contend that the co-operative movement developed in response to popular demand because the consumers were being exploited and that the real pioneers were the workers who built some of the *konsum* stores themselves. They would stress that the movement was built from the bottom up and that they are trustees for the co-operator rather than leaders of the movement. But the fact is that the co-operative movement, like all big business enterprises, is run from the top down and that the Big Seven, who sit on the board of directors, are the driving power in the movement.

For administrative purposes, the country is divided into

twenty-four districts, approximating the provinces of Sweden. Each local co-operative has a vote in the election of a district committee which, in turn, elects the National Congress as well as the members of an administrative council. It is this council which appoints the members of the board of directors of KF.

The administrative council consists of thirty members chosen by the district committees, with at least one member from each district and with two or three representatives from the larger districts. It comprises several members of Parliament, the President of the Stockholm City Council and a number of minor officials, all of them Social Democrats. The council meets at intervals and examines the work of the various branches of KF. It acts as a supervisory organ.

The National Congress is made up of four hundred delegates, elected by the district committees on a basis of proportional representation. It meets twice a year in Stockholm, and its duty is to examine the reports of both the administrative council and the board of directors and to formulate basic policies for guiding the future of the co-operative movement.

The members of the board of directors of KF are nominally elected for two years, but generally hold office until they retire. They are a group of hard-headed businessmen who have made their way up through the ranks and are almost fanatically devoted to the co-operative cause. There is a Swedish expression that they are "all wool," meaning they are solid citizens. They have certain characteristics in common. They are all self-made men. They live a simple, if not austere, life. Several of them came into the movement through the same temperance or religious groups with which the pioneers von Koch, Rylander, and Sundell were associated. They are idealists, yet practical, and they have no desire for personal fortune. All of them could earn more in private business than their salaries as directors of KF. Their salaries are fixed by their own accord at 46,000 crowns a year ($9,200), with the exception of Albin Johansson who, as Chairman of the board, receives 51,000 crowns ($10,200). Johansson has turned down many offers from private business and industry of two or three times that amount.

With the exception of Johansson, who enjoys a wide reputation, the other members of the board are virtually unknown. Only one of them is listed in the Swedish *Who's Who*. And yet each of them has a heavy responsibility. Besides Johansson, the board consists of: Mauritz Bonow, chief brain-truster; Carl Lindskog, in charge of procurement and sale of all foodstuffs, representing over 50 per cent of the entire co-operative business; Gunnar Ekman and John Gillberg, who supervise KF's industries; Hugo Edstam, who looks after clothing and furniture; and Erik Wingard, auditor and contact man between KF and the local societies.

The moving spirit and the real boss is Albin Johansson, who has followed closely in Sundell's footsteps and adhered to his principles. Johansson looks more like a schoolteacher than an alert businessman. He is short by Swedish standards, slightly bent, shabbily dressed, his shaggy wavy hair is graying, and he wears glasses. He talks with emphasis and a confidence which springs from well-earned success. He can be as agreeable as he can be aggressive when the occasion demands. He is a rare combination of a dreamer, an idealist, and a shrewd, even hard-boiled businessman who is both feared and respected. Johansson likes to look forward, not backward. That is one of his strong points, as it is with all the directors of KF. Although none of them are young men, they have a youthful approach. They realize that the continued success of the co-operative movement depends upon the next generation and their own ingenuity in meeting the problems of the future.

Albin Johansson was born in Stockholm sixty-nine years

ago. His father was a mason. He is said to have inherited his aggressiveness from his father and his idealism from his mother, who was quiet, shy, and gentle. Albin started in to work before he even reached his teens. While attending school, at the age of nine, he was running errands for a fruit store and polishing apples. During summer vacations he addressed envelopes for a business firm. He left school when he was thirteen.

Johansson's first steady job was as an errand boy for a Stockholm department store. The store was looking for a couple of boys. Johansson noticed that a well-dressed boy who was in the line-up with his sister immediately obtained one of the jobs. Johansson, who showed an early touch of the shrewdness which has since become so characteristic of him, ran home and returned with his sister. He got the other job.

Once when Johansson was running errands for the department store, he was sent to deliver laundry to Prince Carl, brother of the late King Gustav V. When young Johansson reached the royal estate, he found the Prince and Princess strolling about the garden and went right up to them and delivered his package. Thirty years later Johansson, then well along the road to fame, met Prince Carl. "The last time we met," remarked Johansson with a touch of humor, "was at your estate," remembering the time when he delivered the laundry.

"Yes," replied the Prince, trying to place Johansson in his mind, "we used to have pretty good parties in the old days."

Johansson remained as errand boy with the department store for two years. Various odd jobs in the succeeding years led him, at the age of seventeen, to his first contact with the co-operatives. The Tanto co-operative society, established by workers of a sugar factory in the southern part of Stockholm, needed a clerk. Scores applied for the job and everyone wanted to know what they were going to be paid. But Johansson impressed the manager by asking instead, "What am I supposed to do here?" That got him the job.

Work in the Tanto store was hard. It started at six-thirty in the morning because the men in the adjoining sugar factory came in to buy their snuff before the factory whistle summoned them to work. But Albin did not mind the early hours and has kept them all his life.

From the time he started in to work at Tanto's, the young Johansson showed a keen interest in bookkeeping and figures, which he has maintained to this day. He keeps a personal supervision over the accounts of KF. He has a way of discovering errors that no one else can find. It is Johansson's belief that every school child should have some basic training in economics and business.

Two years after he entered the Tanto store as a clerk, Johansson, then only nineteen, became the store manager. It was as a representative of the store at a co-operative meeting that he first met von Koch and Sundell. He became an intimate friend of both, and it was through this connection that he climbed rapidly to the top of the organization. While he admits that, at the outset, he was only half-hearted about it, he soon became a devoted participant in the movement.

Through this association, Johansson gained a close insight into the whole co-operative field and of the many difficulties which beset the movement in its early days. The main trouble was lack of capital for expansion. In 1907, when Johansson became head of the auditing department, the capital of KF was $30,000, while it is now over $56,000,000. Johansson points proudly to these figures and many other charts which demonstrate the steady growth of KF.

As auditor, Johansson traveled about Sweden, visiting the local societies, lending them a helping hand, reorganizing their bookkeeping, and setting them firmly on their feet. He realized that if the movement were to be the success he envisaged, it had to rest on the financial soundness and prosperity of the local societies.

When Sundell died in 1910, it was natural that his close friend Johansson, who knew his mind better than anyone else, should succeed him as the guiding spirit in the co-operative movement. Johansson, who had the greatest admiration for Sundell, has adhered to his basic principles, while at the same time he has not hesitated to broaden the movement, particularly by entering the industrial field. In 1916 the local co-operatives in Stockholm joined to establish a central *konsum*, and Johansson left KF to become its manager; it was the largest *konsum* in the country. Returning to KF two years later, he became business manager, and in 1924 he was appointed Managing Director of KF and Chairman of the board, a dual position he has held ever since.

Johansson puts in a long day's work, often a ten- or eleven-hour day. He is up every morning at five-thirty when the newspapers are delivered to his home. Although he takes no great interest in world affairs, he reads three newspapers to get the various political viewpoints. The opinionated Social Democratic *Morgon-Tidningen* is essential reading for him. Then he turns to the well-informed liberal *Dagens Nyheter* for a survey of the news and to the conservative *Svenska Dagbladet* for its business columns. At six o'clock he is ready for his first cup of coffee, and at seven he is dressed and in the dining room with his wife for a second cup of coffee and rolls. That is breakfast.

It is three miles from Johansson's home to his office, and he walks the distance morning and evening regardless of weather and seasons. On the occasion of his thirtieth year of service, the board of directors presented him with a car. Johansson listened to the usual eulogy with a sour expression, and when the speaker had finished, he remarked, "I have my salary, that's enough."

But the speaker insisted, "For once, my dear Albin, you are overruled and outvoted." Johansson accepted reluctantly, but has never used the car.

Johansson is among the first to reach work at eight-thirty in the morning, and he is among the last to leave, often as late as seven o'clock at night. His office, as Managing Director, is a large front room on the seventh floor of KF headquarters, facing the Stockholm waterfront. There are six big windows, and Johansson likes to leave them open as much as possible, summer and winter. The thick pall of smoke from his incessant cigar smoking makes it necessary to air the room at frequent intervals. Johansson's eight-cent cigars are famous among KF workers. He smokes ten of them a day and has been doing it for over forty years.

From Johansson's office, a majestic sweep of the eye takes in the whole of the city, from the golden steeple of the City Hall surmounted by the crest of the three crowns to the left, to the estate of the late Prince Eugen, a brother of the late King Gustav V—now a public park—far off to the right across the waters of Stockholm Bay. It is a constantly changing scene from the long summer days and short nights when the sun barely dips below the horizon, silhouetting Stockholm's medieval church steeples against the glow of a crimson sky, to the darkness of winter when the city lights cast a dull reflection in the frozen canals. This is one of the world's great sights, and Johansson never tires of it. This hardheaded businessman is enough of a dreamer not to be unresponsive to the beauties of nature.

Johansson's desk is to the left as you enter. But he rarely uses it. He prefers instead to sit alone at a long table in the center of the room where he can scatter his papers around him, for tidiness is not one of Johansson's strong points. The exemplary efficiency throughout the KF organization does not extend to his personal habits.

On the wall behind his desk hangs an eighteenth-century tapestry, a conventional subject—a pair of lovers with a cherub bearing a basket of fruit. There are a couple of similar tapestries on other walls and some indifferent modern paintings. Johansson says quite frankly that they are not pieces of art but that he keeps them out of "pious consideration" because they were given him on special occasions, such as his fiftieth birthday. There are also portraits of the original board members of KF, and on a bookcase there is a small bronze bust of Martin Sundell.

Johansson is a trouble-shooter. KF is so organized that only the really big issues reach the top executives. Other problems are settled at lower levels. KF is said to accord the lower echelons the greatest latitude and initiative in any line of Swedish business. Routine problems never reach Johansson and his board. Johansson decides most of the big issues, and when he cannot settle them, he takes them to the board, which meets every Wednesday for the entire day. The items for the board meeting are registered in a special book on Johansson's desk. There are usually thirty or forty items scheduled for discussion at each meeting.

Johansson believes that it is not enough for the co-operatives to be on a level with Sweden's big business, but that they must be one step ahead. This calls for constant planning. "KF has built up the best business organization in Sweden," Johansson says proudly. "But that isn't enough. The others have copied our methods and are always catching up on us. That means that we have to do better."

When Johansson is at work, he wastes no time. Two secretaries keep his appointments and shield him from unwanted callers. He takes only fifteen minutes off for lunch in the KF dining room two floors above his office. There are three lunch periods for KF employees, and Johansson takes his during the third period between twelve-fifteen and one o'clock. The dining room seats sixty employees at five long tables. Johansson has no special seat, and the Managing Director may well be lunching alongside an office boy.

The lunch fare is simple. For fourteen cents KF employees have a two-course lunch. It may consist of a plate of soup—cabbage soup is a favorite—with a meat ball, followed by rice pudding and a fruit sauce, a slice or two of bread with margarine from KF's own factory, and the choice of a cup of tea, coffee, or milk. It is self-service, and there is no loitering. Lunch is only a necessary and brief interval in the day's work.

It is early to rise but also early to bed for Johansson. He could be out to dinner every night but he limits his engagements to a couple a week, and then he leaves the party long ahead of the other guests.

Besides his grueling work at KF, Johansson fills a number of important positions. He is a member of the Board of the State Railways and of the Swedish tobacco monopoly. He served as a member of the Board of the Royal Opera for seventeen years, eight of them as President of the board. He admits, however, that he has little interest in opera—that his contribution was solely on the business side. Opera in Sweden, as in most countries, has been on a deficit basis, and Johansson's job was to keep it, in so far as possible, out of the red. His favorite program is a rarely played operetta, *The Girl of the Golden West*.

Swimming is Johansson's principal hobby. He has always been a good swimmer, but it was not until after he turned sixty that he qualified for a master's degree. He took the test three times, gaining in succession the bronze, silver, and gold medals. This is probably unprecedented at Johansson's age. The test consists of a two-mile swim—one mile, fully clothed. It also calls for a twenty-five-yard swim under water and five successive dives to a depth of fifteen feet. As a final requirement there is a 300-yard swim treading water. Johansson boasts that he took these tests at the end of the day's work and without cutting down on his cigar smoking.

Johansson has another hobby, too. He is President of the Inventors' Society. He never tires of listening to inventors, no matter what crank ideas they may have. Several of his own devices have been adopted by KF. These are gadgets for office and factory use.

Practical as he is in matters of business, Johansson is an idealist when it comes to international affairs. He wants tariff barriers abolished and would like to start with the Scandinavian countries. But beyond that, he urges a division of the world's natural resources on the co-operative principle. He considers that competition for raw materials is a prime factor in promoting wars, and that if all states could gain an equitable share of the world's resources, the danger of conflict would be greatly minimized, if not eliminated. But he does not explain how this can be brought about. Perhaps Johansson feels that he can afford to dream, since he is practical enough to know that this will not occur in his lifetime.

Although the retirement age in KF, as in most other Swedish businesses, is fixed at sixty-seven, it has been decided that Albin Johansson, whose position is unique, shall continue until 1957, when he will be seventy-one years of age.

The man closest to Johansson is Mauritz Bonow, Secretary General of KF, who is mainly responsible for shaping the future of the co-operative movement. While Johansson wrestles with the immediate problems and dreams about the future, Bonow actually plans it.

Bonow was virtually born into the movement. His father

had been an engine driver, but in his later years the older Bonow became interested in the co-operatives and was a member of the Central Co-operative Committee in Luleå.

Mauritz Bonow, though self-made, has more of an education than most of the other members of the board. He graduated from Uppsala University in 1930, writing his thesis on the fight between the cartels and the co-operatives, a fight in which he was to play a leading part in the years to follow. He has called it "a war against private monopoly."

Unlike other members of the KF board, Bonow did not climb from the bottom up, but entered the organization near the top as an assistant to the Publicity Director, a position he later came to fill and has held for the past fourteen years. This is one of the most important functions in the co-operative organization, for KF leaders realize fully that if the movement is to continue growing, the masses must be educated in its principles.

Bonow's official title is Director of Education, and his duties are so numerous that it is difficult to conceive how any one man can fill them all. These are some of the tasks he performs: he keeps the statutes of the organization and sees that they are revised when needed; he supervises the co-operative school which trains personnel for executive positions; he conducts a correspondence school which is operated jointly under the auspices of the trade unions and the co-operatives; he is the publisher of the popular co-operative weekly magazine *Vi* (*We*), also the co-operative household organ *Kooperatören*. He supervises three publishing firms: The Co-operative Publishing Company, which specializes in books on economics and social welfare; Rabén & Sjögren, publishers of children's books; and Ehlin's School Material Publishing Company, which provides textbooks for adults interested in economics and the co-operative movement.

Notwithstanding this impressive list of duties, Bonow finds

time to talk leisurely with visitors, giving the impression that he has almost nothing to do. A stocky, middle-aged, balding man, Bonow sits calmly at his desk, which is clear of papers, smokes an occasional cigarette, and looks out unconcernedly over the famous view of Stockholm Bay in a manner indicating that he has become indifferent to the scene beyond. He throws a switch so that the telephone is answered in his outer office and he is barricaded from the public and his own staff. The Bonow pattern of efficiency is followed on the executive level throughout the KF organization.

But despite his apparent aloofness, Bonow is more deeply immersed in the movement than anyone else except Albin Johansson. He is completely devoted to it. And like the other directors, he admits that he is not in it for money and has no interest in personal wealth. Only recently Bonow treated himself to the luxury of a small Swedish car, and his ambition is to own a rowboat.

Bonow admits he has a hard job but he says it isn't a killing one. And to prove it, he points to the portraits of his ten predecessors, which hang on his office wall, eight of whom are still alive, and he thinks that speaks for itself. The oldest portrait is one of pioneer von Koch, and the latest is that of Axel Gjöres, former Minister of Trade.

I questioned Bonow about the long-range future of the co-operative movement in Sweden. If the co-operatives should invade an increasing number of industrial spheres, I asked him, would it not tend to establish a totalitarian economy? Bonow's answer was categorical. The Swedish co-operatives, he said, do not aim to take over any industry completely. On the contrary, they are fighting the private monopolies and do not intend to substitute another type of monopoly. The co-operatives want to reduce prices for the benefit of the consumer, he explained, by driving a sufficient wedge into a particular industry to break the price level. This can be done, according to Bonow, by controlling from 15 to 25 per cent of that industry.

When the co-operatives have achieved their purpose in lowering the price level, Bonow explained further, they consider that their goal has been reached. If the co-operatives make a profit, as they invariably do, they set it aside as capital to enable them to enter other fields. Bonow emphasized that there is no intention of driving out private business and that the co-operatives welcome competition. Of course, private business has another story to tell.

Bonow believes that a co-operative movement can only flourish in a free country. Hitler, he says, made a farce of the German co-operative movement, using it as a mere tool of the totalitarian system, and the same is true in Russia and the satellite states. The success of the co-operative movement, he contends, rests entirely with the people, and it can only function in countries where the people have a free say. Bonow is for a minimum of Government restrictions and a free economy which, he believes, affords the co-operative movement the greatest scope.

Looking to the future, Bonow considers that KF can expand in two ways. It can continue to open up new co-operative stores throughout the country and it can branch out into new industries. The co-operative stores are now responsible for between 20 and 25 per cent of the total retail food business in Sweden, and Bonow believes this can be stepped up to between 30 and 40 per cent. He does not go along with those enthusiasts who aim to take over from 50 to 75 per cent of the food business—he wants the consumers to continue to have the choice between the co-operatives and the private stores. As for expansion into industrial fields, Bonow sees no limit. He would have KF enter any new field in which it feels the consumer is being exploited.

The man who handles the important food department and

its distribution to the 8,077 co-operative stores throughout the country is Carl Lindskog, who has been connected with the co-operatives for a quarter of a century and has become one of Sweden's foremost agricultural experts, serving on various government committees.

Lindskog came to the local co-operative in Malmö, in south Sweden, looking for a job during the depression of the early twenties, and was fortunate enough to step in as a substitute clerk, helping clear foreign goods through customs. His knowledge of English and German served him so well that he kept the job. He later became a salesman for KF and traveled throughout Sweden, cultivating a relationship with the local societies and stores which was to prove useful throughout his career. His travels also took him abroad as a buyer to Greece, Turkey, and Yugoslavia. It was hard going, and Lindskog advanced arduously step by step until he became head of the foreign food department and three years ago was appointed a member of the board.

Now in his fifties, Lindskog is short, chubby, vital, even dynamic. He does the thinking and planning and leaves the carrying out of the projects to others. "I have an excellent team of workers," he explains. "They are responsible for their own departments. They buy and sell, and I expect them to show results—what we call a 'surplus,' since we do not use the word 'profit.' It is only when they do not produce that I have to do something about it."

But there are many problems of policy that keep Lindskog busy. The food business is undergoing a revolution, with people turning increasingly to semiprepared and ready foods and new mechanical household equipment. Lindskog is now trying to convince Albin Johansson and the leaders of co-operative societies in the country that the young people are reaching out for a higher standard of living and that they want the new household equipment and can afford it. The more conservative members of the board are hesitant to go along with him, in the belief that youth should not be encouraged to waste its money in lavish expenditure. Lindskog's comment is that the co-operative movement must remain young and that when he reaches sixty, he is going to retire from the board and leave the job to a younger man.

It is Lindskog personally who started the co-operatives in the farming business. He bought the sixty-acre farm near Malmö as an experiment to see how cheaply vegetables can be produced, and it is his war with the farmer. Vegetables, principally tomatoes and cucumbers, from Paradise Farm— as the co-operative farm is known—are now being sold at cut-rate prices in co-operative food stores throughout Sweden. But how much of a dent this will eventually make on the farmers' co-operatives is yet too early to predict.

Adjoining Lindskog's office at KF headquarters is a special laboratory for testing foods. There experts make a careful study, comparing co-operative products with those of competing firms. Most of these are canned foods. Every tin is carefully weighed and its contents checked with competitive products to see that the co-operative client receives the most for his money. The motto is: "Maintain the quality and lower the price."

Lindskog is a fighter. Some compare him to the pioneer Sundell. He expresses his creed in these terms: "We must remain fresh. We must do our best every minute of the hour and every hour of the day. What we turn out must be cheap, profitable, modern, and effective."

As head of KF's food department, Lindskog supervises eight factories: the famous margarine factory which was the first built by the co-operatives in 1920 in the opening battle against the big business cartels, a vegetable-oil factory, three flour mills, a marmalade factory, a fruit-canning plant, and a seafood cannery.

But most of KF's industries come under the over-all supervision of two men: Gunnar Ekman, who is in charge of heavy industry, and John Gillberg, who looks after light industry. Ekman supervises forty-eight factories, while Gillberg operates thirteen different commodity branches; both represent KF's interest in a score of other enterprises. Neither has ever had time to figure out how many industries they control respectively.

Ekman joined the co-operative rubber factory at Gislaved thirty years ago and has been associated with commodity production ever since. At one time it was bicycles, and later he became manager of the Stathmos factory, manufacturing scales. Under his successful management the factory doubled its production and developed an export market in thirty-five countries, including the United States, where Stathmos scales are used in a hospital in Houston, Texas. It was his successful operation of the Stathmos factory that brought him a two-line note from Albin Johansson, notifying him of his appointment as a member of the board to co-ordinate industry.

"Our policy," says Ekman, "is to concentrate on the production of consumer goods, but there are exceptions. For instance, we have gone into the making of nitrogen for the farmer in order to lower the price of foodstuffs. It is difficult to draw the line. There is certainly a great possibility for industrial expansion, but it is not as easy as it used to be, since it now requires large initial investment. We do not want to establish any monopoly, but we are strong enough to give the consumer the right price."

KF's latest challenge is its attempt to cut the price of washing powder. Under Ekman's guidance, KF is now producing a new powdered soap, Sulfo, the price of which is 30 per cent below that of its closest competitor. But although the Sulfo factory is working three shifts, day and night, KF has not succeeded in breaking the price level, and competitors are still selling their wares at prices from one-third to twice as high. But it is a fight which KF is determined to push to a successful finish.

Ekman says the increase in co-operative membership during the past year, when 21,000 new members joined the movement, is due in large part to the housewife's satisfaction with Sulfo and the realization that the co-operatives are fighting for lower prices. He claims that Swedish housewives are not attracted by the extravagant advertising offers of competing imports which "offer your weight in gold to answer a simple question," but prefer a cheaper-priced product.

Gillberg is something of a revolutionary within the movement. He feels that Sundell's principles were all right in his day when KF was only a small business, but that nowadays big business cannot be conducted solely on a cash basis and that KF must make loans and allow members to pay for commodity purchases by easy payment methods.

KF has got around both of these difficulties without directly sacrificing the Sundell principles. It still insists on cash payments, but the Co-operative Savings Bank now extends loans to buyers of expensive commodities, such as sewing machines, vacuum cleaners, refrigerators, bicycles, cash registers, etc., enabling them to pay cash and repay the bank in installments. There are three conditions: buyers must be members of a co-operative society; must be at least twenty-one years of age; and must be employed. The loan is offered without security, and KF guarantees it. It is repaid in ten installments during the year, excepting December, the Christmas month, and July, the vacation season, and the interest is 6 per cent, but it is refunded if the installments are paid on time.

In 1952, KF made the other exception. It issued a unique type of loan for subscription by co-operative members. It is a twenty-year loan at 3 per cent interest, and KF promises to pay compensation for any depreciation in the value of the Swedish currency up to 50 per cent of the face value of the bond when it matures, based on the official index in the cost of living. The index is published annually and is an important factor in fixing wage agreements.

Gillberg explains that this is not exactly contrary to Sundell's no-loan policy since it is a family affair among co-operative members and no money is borrowed from the outside. The loan was subscribed up to 70,000,000 crowns ($14,000,000).

Clothing and furniture also account for a large share of KF's business, and this branch comes under the supervision of Hugo Edstam, who also runs the PUB department store in Stockholm. Edstam is a progressive businessman with a strict religious background. He is a singer in the church choir, a Sunday-school teacher, and a temperance advocate. It was the conservative character of the co-operatives, he relates, that first attracted him to the movement. He had heard that the co-operatives served no liquor at their meetings and that directors were paid low salaries. In his youthful days these seemed to be good points, but Edstam admits that he was idealistic then and that he would not mind if the directors' salaries were higher now.

Edstam was the son of a poor storekeeper who failed in business at the time of World War I. He was then only fifteen years of age and was compelled to go to work. He rose from errand boy to traveling salesman, and then became head of the advertising department of a shoe factory in the town of Örebro in central Sweden. KF established a competitive factory and enticed Edstam to join by offering him a ten-dollar-a-month raise. That made all the difference at the time because Edstam was just planning to get married.

Much of the modern furniture so popular in middle-class and workers homes throughout Sweden is the product of the co-operatives. It is plain, cheap, neat, and bright. Edstam knows that it is unpopular with older people and constantly receives complaints from them. They would prefer the heavier, ornate copies of period furniture. But Edstam is practical. He knows that the modern furniture, with plain lines and in light woods, can be molded more easily and produced at much lower prices. Furthermore, Edstam is looking ahead, and he is convinced that the youth of Sweden wants the modern furniture because it is more practical and economical.

The youngest member of the board of KF is Erik Wingard, 50, who has the important post of auditor, once held by Albin Johansson. The title is misleading because Wingard's job involves far more than auditing and bookkeeping, and he is mainly responsible for keeping up the ties between KF and the co-operative societies in the country. On this solidarity rests the whole structure of the co-operative movement.

According to KF rules, no new society can be established anywhere in Sweden without the approval of the auditing department at KF headquarters in Stockholm, meaning that Wingard's consent is necessary before any new society can come into existence. This gives him a wide degree of control over the growth and development of the co-operative movement. Local societies are required, furthermore, to submit accounts to the auditing department of KF at regular intervals, so that Wingard has the entire business of the co-operatives at his fingertips.

The district auditors throughout the country who report to Wingard have also much wider authority than might be supposed. They advise the local societies, plan their expansion, and are responsible for carrying on KF's campaign to educate the people regarding the co-operative movement. They also select promising candidates among district personnel for special schooling and eventual executive jobs in KF.

Like most other members of the board, Wingard came from a poor family. His father was a fisherman and two of his five brothers are fishermen. Wingard had only six years of schooling before he went to sea, and had no other ambition than to follow in the family footsteps. His love of the sea has endured to this day, and whenever he gets a chance, he slips away to the West Coast for a fishing trip with his brothers.

A fisherman's life is never easy, but nature has contrived to make it doubly hazardous along Sweden's rocky West Coast, particularly in the winter months when the gales blow in from the North Sea and lash at the flimsy fishing villages, huddled on the barren, treeless rocks. These simple wooden frame houses seem as if they had been tossed up by the sea in its fury and dropped at random on the rocky ledges of the jagged coast.

In autumn and winter the Wingards would go far out in the North Sea in their small sailing vessel for a week or two at a time to fish for herring, battling storms, snow, fog, and ice. When spring came at last, they would cast their nets along the coast for mackerel, which is salted and exported to Germany and the United States.

Forlorn and desolate as the fishing villages are in the winter, they come cheerfully to life in the summer when visitors from the cities swarm to the seashore, relax on the sun-drenched rocks, and look out lazily over the placid blue expanse of water, dotted with the sails of pleasure craft. In the evenings the people gather on the pier to listen or dance to the tunes of an accordion played by some old fisherman. This is only a brief interlude for the fishing folk, who overhaul their boats in preparation for the next season.

In the days of Wingard's youth, these fishing communities were staunchly conservative. The people were influenced by a religious awakening, a deeply rooted temperance movement, and by a stirring of the labor forces that was to lead Sweden far in a progressive direction and was to provide a stimulus for the development of the co-operative movement. These forces were closely interwoven in the fabric of the community. Wingard joined the temperance movement at the age of seventeen, and through it came into the co-operative movement. He went to work in a co-operative store in a fishing community on an island off the West Coast. It was one of the first co-operatives established among fishermen and enabled them to obtain their tackle and other supplies at low cost. Seven years later, Wingard was selected for a training course at the co-operative school which led to a job in the accounting department at KF headquarters in Stockholm, where he has been ever since.

Wingard shows no signs of his modest background. He is physically well built, tall, and sturdy. His manner is polished, he is an easy talker, and is perhaps the best-dressed member of the board and the most cosmopolitan.

To obtain Wingard's recognition, any new co-operative society must start with a minimum capital of $2,000. If the group wants to build its own store rather than rent space, it must put up at least $20,000, for Wingard insists on sufficient capital to minimize any risk of failure.

Capital may be raised in various ways: through regular bank loans; through KF's "rescue" organization, which is ready to lend a helping hand if Wingard thinks the prospects are good; or from a neighboring co-operative, now the most common practice. The day when local societies had to struggle to their own feet is past. If Wingard gives his approval, the new society is assured of KF's backing, directly or indirectly.

When Wingard was a pupil at the co-operative training school, he recalls that one of the trick questions asked was, "Should the co-operatives fight luxury?" Most of the class answered in the affirmative, but the right answer was, "What is luxury?" To Wingard, luxury is the pinnacle he has now reached.

The seven members of the board of directors of KF are as shrewd and seasoned a group of business executives as can be found anywhere in Sweden. They plan aggressively and even ruthlessly, with an abundant confidence in the future of the movement they direct.

CHAPTER V

More Co-operation

AMONG its many functions, KF carries on what the leaders of the movement call an education campaign which is actually extensive propaganda to acquaint Swedish consumers with the benefits they may expect from the co-operatives. From the outset co-operative leaders recognized that the success of the movement depended upon the support of the masses and that this called for spreading the co-operative message by every available means, including advertising, films, public-speaking, publishing, and educational training.

Herman Stolpe, head of KF's publishing activities, has said that the Swedish co-operative movement "can only gain in strength and influence if its membership is permeated with a sound economic insight which facilitates an appraisal of the co-operative movement in relation to the economic life." Accordingly, co-operative leaders have conducted their propaganda on extremely broad lines by attempting to educate the public in general economics, in the belief that such a knowledge will contribute to a higher standard of living and indirectly benefit the co-operative movement.

Propagandists have coined a number of appealing slogans. The motto of the movement is: "Co-operate to gain *for* and not *from* each other." Other slogans are "Unity is strength" and "In our own hands," meaning that the co-operatives belong to the masses. Every co-operative society and store in Sweden displays a poster showing three violets growing straight out of the earth. This poster, which bears the legend, "From arid soil," was designed for the fiftieth anniversary of the co-operative movement and is intended to show that the movement grew from a solid foundation among the people. The purple color is that of the banner of the International Co-operative Alliance.

The co-operative message is spread through study groups organized among local co-operative societies, by correspondence courses, and by the co-operative training school at Saltsjöbaden, a resort close to Stockholm. All these activities are closely related and are intended mainly for co-operative personnel.

The co-operative training-school prepares employees for executive jobs in the local societies as well as in KF headquarters. It was established a quarter of a century ago, and 1,500 pupils now take the courses annually. The courses vary from a brief training period of several weeks for shop clerks from local *konsum* stores to a two-year period for promising candidates for executive positions in the co-operative movement. The school is located in an old English-style country house, formerly owned by a prominent Swedish banker. The original *konsum* store operated by the pioneer Martin Sundell is preserved on the grounds as a museum.

The school is run by Harald Elldin, a former Social Democratic member of Parliament, who was prominent in the labor movement. Elldin has a common-sense approach and believes in putting co-operative theories into practice. Students are taught the basic co-operative principles and are given courses in salesmanship, window dressing, furnishing, bookkeeping, and in the many useful tasks connected with running a successful store. The courses are extremely simple, but Elldin realizes that the needs of the country stores are simple and the co-operative movement is patterned to the popular demand.

Students pay no tuition fee but, on the contrary, receive a salary of approximately $80 a month while attending the courses. This is to make up for their loss in pay during this period. They receive no diploma at the termination of the course, but they are assured of a better job and they frequently return from the longer courses to fill jobs with a 50 per cent raise in pay. The cost of operating the school is defrayed by KF and amounts to about $100,000 annually.

KF's main organ is the weekly magazine *Vi,* which has a circulation of 600,000, the largest in Sweden, but this is because all co-operative societies subscribe to it in bulk for their members. Although it is sold mostly by subscription, it is also available on the newsstands. The subscription price is only $1.60 a year, or seven cents a copy. The cost of publication is paid largely from a special fund of 1 per cent of KF's total turnover, which is set aside yearly for propaganda. *Vi* appeals to workers and particularly to women. It contains articles of general interest about Sweden, but with the co-operative or labor angle uppermost.

The biweekly household organ *Kooperatören* is circulated to 15,000 employees of the co-operatives and contains editorials about the movement, sketches of personalities, and quotations from co-operative leaders. Albin Johansson's sayings appear over and over again. In his absent-minded way Johansson has been known to underscore and comment on some of his own contributions without remembering the authorship.

KF, which operates three publishing firms, is one of the

largest publishers of low-cost books in Sweden, and produces approximately 150 books annually, mainly on economic subjects. Its bestsellers include such heavy reading as *National Economy for All* by Professor Silverstolpe. The co-operatives have joined with Norstedt and Sons, one of Sweden's leading publishers, and established the Wing Publishing House to produce large editions of popular novels by well-known Swedish and foreign authors without profit. This is part of the co-operative program to raise the intellectual level of the masses. The private firm chose this profitless partnership rather than face the competition of KF.

The wide activities of KF include a co-operative savings bank. Members of the co-operative movement can make deposits and withdraw funds through the local societies. The societies deposit their funds in the regular commercial banks, but they are earmarked for the account of KF, which invests them to earn an interest of 1 per cent more than the usual bank rate. This has aroused a great deal of opposition on the part of the banks, which have contended that the Co-operative Savings Bank should be subject to the same regulations as other banks, but the Government has ignored this protest.

KF is also in the insurance business. It controls two large insurance companies which have been brought together under joint management. In 1908 KF established a fire-insurance company, known as *Samarbete* (Co-operation) and six years later a life-insurance society, *Folket* (the People). As Swedish law prohibits one company from dealing in both types of insurance, the two companies have been kept technically separate, but they are operated by the same board of directors appointed by the Administrative Council of KF. The joint companies are popularly known as *Folksam,* and they handle business in excess of $80,000,000 a year.

Folksam has 2,000,000 policyholders. Besides fire and life insurance, it now handles marine insurance, and the largest part of its business consists of collective accident insurance placed by the trade unions or groups of workers, covering 1,800,000 members of the labor force, a total exceeding the membership of the Confederation of Trade Unions. This insurance supplements the benefits under the compulsory health insurance, which covers all sickness and accident cases up to ninety days of treatment. It carries the insurance further and is for the most part compulsory.

As a result of the new compulsory health insurance, which brings medical care to the entire population, *Folksam* lowered its rates on life insurance twice during 1955. It now offers $20,000 worth of life insurance for an average of thirty cents a day. The ninety-day free medical care now offered by the State also enabled *Folksam* to cut its accident rate by 28 per cent. *Folksam* still manages to make a substantial profit, most of which is set aside in a reserve fund to meet hard times should they arise. This fund amounted to $84,-000,000 at the close of 1954.

Over 80 per cent of the assets of *Folksam* are invested in building operations and, in particular, in co-operative undertakings. It lends funds to co-operative stores for improvement of their property, to the Co-operative Household Society for new developments, and for the building of community halls for the benefit of the labor groups. Every town and village in Sweden has at least one community hall which is the social center for the working classes. *Folksam* goes on the principle that since most of its policyholders are laborers, the company's first obligation is to provide better homes and a better life for the workers.

The co-operatives benefit from certain advantages in taxation. They are classified as economic societies which, under a law passed by the Swedish Parliament in 1947, fixes the State tax rate at 32 per cent of their profits, as compared to the regular 40 per cent for corporations. KF is rated as an economic society in the same way as the local co-operatives, but since its business is many times greater, it is the principal beneficiary of the cut in the tax rate. Factories operated by KF, however, are established as joint stock companies and receive no special treatment.

Another advantage derived by the co-operatives is that the dividend paid to members at the end of each year, generally about 3 per cent but in some cases running as high as 8 per cent, is tax-free. It is considered a refund on purchases rather than a profit. The co-operative dividend is looked upon as a public service.

Property owned by the co-operatives is also tax-free, whereas private firms and individuals pay a tax on all property in excess of a value of $6,000. Co-operative leaders insist that they have never attempted to gain special favors in taxation, and confusing tables are produced to show that at certain low levels the co-operatives pay as much in taxes as private business. However, with few exceptions the laws favor the co-operatives, and particularly the larger societies and KF itself. These concessions, voted by Parliament, are part of the program favoring labor.

Even more extensive than the consumer co-operatives, though less well known, are the farmers' co-operatives. Some 300,000 Swedish farmers—virtually all those who offer their produce for sale—belong to the Federation of Swedish Farmers' Associations, the central co-operative authority, while 75 per cent belong to the Farmers' Union, which is closely affiliated. A few figures serve to illustrate the scope of the farmers' co-operative movement. The federation's annual turnover amounts to $400,000,000; it operates 640 dairies, 60 slaughterhouses, 40 meat factories, 100 distilleries, and provides 500 warehouses for storage purposes. It handles 87 per cent of all the farm produce of Sweden.

Farmers who belong to the co-operative movement can devote almost all their time and effort to cultivating their crops and raising their cattle. All the problems of marketing their products and of transportation and distribution are taken out of their hands. The various local co-operative organizations take delivery of the farmer's produce and also slaughter his cattle. He is paid regularly by the co-operatives at a price fixed by the farm organizations in conjunction with the Government. The slogan of the agricultural co-operatives is: "The same price for the same quality and no exceptions."

The agricultural co-operative movement had its beginning in Sweden about the same time as the consumers' co-operative movement, toward the end of the last century. As in the case of the consumers' co-operatives, the agricultural societies developed locally at first and faced great difficulties. Many of them went bankrupt in the depression of the twenties. This led to a more determined effort at co-operation and to the establishment in 1930 of the Federation of Swedish Farmers' Associations, which marked a turning point for the farmers and the rise of the agricultural co-operatives as a dominant factor in Sweden's rural economy.

The federation embraces twelve national organizations and 140 affiliated provincial societies. The setup is complex, even more intricate than that of the consumers' co-operatives, with greater emphasis on the local societies. In the first place, there is the local agricultural society, which is a unit of a provincial society. The latter is a member of one of the dozen national organizations representing the principal branches of the agricultural industry which are joined in the federation, the central authority. The board of twenty directors of the federation is chosen by the seven largest organizations and by members of a national congress. Inasmuch as the local societies have direct contact with the farmers and collect, process and sell their products within the area, there is much more decentralization than in the case of the consumers' co-operatives, which look to KF for almost everything. The farmers' co-operative movement is built from the bottom up.

The largest of the national organizations are the dairy and meat-marketing associations. The Swedish Dairies Association, with 250,000 members, handles 97.6 per cent of all milk and butter sold in Swedish dairies and 94.1 per cent of all cheese. The organization has an annual turnover of $200,-000,000. It collects the milk from the farmers in its own trucks. The farmer places the milk containers along the route, and they are returned to him with whatever butter and cheese he may have ordered from the association. Few farmers produce their own butter and cheese.

The Meat Marketing Association, with 270,000 members, controls three-quarters of all the meat produced in Sweden. It slaughters the cattle, markets the meat, and sells the hides. The farmer delivers his cattle to the slaughterhouse and the association looks after the rest of the business.

The other key national organizations include: a purchasing and selling association for the marketing of vegetables; associations for egg marketing, forestry, fur breeding, starch products, distillers, flax and hemp growers, oil plant cultivation; credit and mortgage societies to help the farmers with their financial problems. Membership in any of these organizations carries with it automatic membership in the over-all federation.

The cost of membership in the different societies varies considerably and is on a percentage basis. For instance, the Dairies Association charges six dollars for every 200 gallons of milk delivered by the farmer, while the meat association, curiously enough, charges on a percentage of the grazing area rather than per head of cattle. The farmer does not have to pay the fee in cash, but it may be deducted from his pay check from the local co-operative. Thus every farmer can afford the membership fee.

The head of the Federation of Swedish Farmers' Associations is Einar Sjögren, who is Chairman of the board and Managing Director. Sjögren is a practical farmer, a scientific one, and a politician. He was born in the same year as Albin Johansson, sixty-nine years ago. His father owned a small farm in southern Sweden, and young Sjögren started working on it at the age of seven and continued throughout his school years whenever he had an opportunity.

Sjögren graduated from the Agricultural College at Ultuna, near Stockholm, and became a farm expert. He worked as a farm inspector on large estates in the rich farming district of southern Sweden, returning sixteen years later to the Agricultural College as a director. The college is conducted along practical lines, and the students gain their experience on a thousand-acre farm.

In 1937 Sjögren was elected a member of the Lower House of the Swedish Parliament on a Conservative ticket, where he served for four years. The farm owners in Sweden generally belong to the Farmers' or Conservative parties, which are classed as rightist parties. The bulk of the farm laborers, however, belong to the Social Democratic Party.

Sjögren is a heavy-set, square-shouldered man of the soil, with ruddy complexion and graying hair. Though genial and hearty, he believes in using few words. A placard framed on the wall behind his desk carries this legend: "A wise old owl lived in an oak tree. The more it saw, the less it talked. The less it talked, the more it heard. Why can't we be like that wise old owl?"

The federation occupies only a small office in down-town Stockholm, along newspaper row. Unlike KF, the farmers' central organization is not the directive force in the movement. It is rather a co-ordinating agency which serves to

bring together the many branches. Sjögren's main task, and
it is a most important one, is to negotiate an annual agreement with the Government regulating the price of farm
products. He speaks for virtually all the farmers in Sweden.

Einar Sjögren, head of the farmers' co-operatives, and Albin Johansson, boss of the consumers' co-operatives, have
little in common. They are, as Sjögren admits plainly, in
competition. Attempts over many years to bring about some
definite understanding between the two great organizations
they represent have failed repeatedly. The trouble is that
Johansson is fighting for low prices for the consumers and
Sjögren wants prices that will assure the farmers a better
living. KF has now acquired a large farm in southern Sweden
and is growing vegetables experimentally to determine how
low prices can be set. This is a challenge which is being
watched nervously by the farmers.

The consumers' co-operatives have long posed as the friend
of the Swedish farmer, ready to help him with the tools and
the implements necessary for his trade. Actually, KF factories do supply the farmers with fertilizers and with certain
farming implements. But Sjögren makes this caustic comment: "The farmers' co-operatives fear the consumers' co-
operatives even when they come bearing gifts."

Sjögren, however, believes that someday an agreement
will be worked out which will delimit the spheres of the two
co-operatives. In the meantime, a general agreement, negotiated in 1945 but which failed to obtain the necessary 75
per cent support on the part of the farmers, is being observed. It calls for fixing "the lowest possible margin between
the price the farmer obtains for his products and which the
consumer pays," while KF pledges to help farmers attain a
living standard equivalent to the other labor groups. Attempts to draw a line whereby the farmers would look after
the farming end only while the consumers' co-operatives

would take over the marketing have failed. Swedish farmers are determined to keep their business in their own hands.

Sjögren gave up politics twenty years ago when he became head of the nonpolitical Federation of Swedish Farmers' Associations, but he did not give up farming. He has a forty-acre farm in the neighborhood of Stockholm where he spends his leisure time. It is a modern mechanized farm where Sjögren applies the theories he has been teaching in the Agricultural College. Asked if he makes a profit, he says, "I do all right."

For the most part Sweden is a country of small farms. Two-thirds of its 300,000 farms consist of less than twenty-five acres of cultivable land, and these farmers make ends meet by tilling the soil themselves with members of their family. Owners of farms of between 25 and 125 acres derive a relatively good income, while the 7,000 owners of large farms, in excess of 125 acres, earn a substantial profit.

I have visited a number of farms in Sweden in all the three categories, searching for the average farmer. Such a farmer is Hugo Pettersson of Enby, thirty miles south of Stockholm. He owns forty acres of cultivable land; fifty acres of forest-land; eight cows; ten calves; two pigs; a horse; and a sufficient number of chickens for his own use. He and his wife and their twenty-one-year-old daughter, Ingegerd, look after the farm. They have no other help.

Pettersson's farm is perched on a hilltop, dominating an undulating valley. It is an old farm which has remained in the Pettersson family for two centuries, and they are proud of the heritage. They feel they have a tradition behind them and a duty to uphold it. The Petterssons are conservative and are outraged by the fact that a neighboring farmer is a Communist. Their farm consists of four buildings: the Pettersson home; the former home dating back to the eighteenth century which is now used as a storehouse; and two sheds, one for the animals and the other for the storage of grain. The Pettersson home is a white wooden two-story house, with a large drawing room, combination office and dining room, and a modern kitchen on the ground floor. There are three bedrooms upstairs. It is plainly furnished but is scrupulously clean, and there are carefully trained potted plants in the corners of the drawing room. The general impression is one of comfort and ease, though not of luxury. The storehouse and the barns are painted a dark red with a white frame border, characteristic of the Swedish countryside.

Farmer Pettersson is a sturdy, weather-beaten man. He is interested in his crops and his cattle. His wife is tall, lanky, and energetic. She runs the household. Their daughter is the business manager, and she keeps the books, makes out the tax reports, helps with the harvest, and can fill any job on the farm. Someday it will be hers to carry on. The Petterssons are friendly and hospitable, and they are quite willing to talk about the farm and their problems.

The soil is only fair and there is always some uncertainty about the crops. It is not the rich soil of southern Sweden nor the chalky, barren soil of the northern part of the country. It is just average farmland, and a long winter means poor crops, although the Petterssons face no hardship on that account. They have an assured income from milk and cattle-raising.

The Petterssons grow hay, oats, and beets as fodder for the cattle. There are four acres of potatoes and four acres of wheat. The fodder suffices only for Pettersson's own cattle, and the potatoes and wheat are sold. Pettersson's main source of income is from milk. His eight cows produce 10,000 gallons of milk a year and bring in an income of $2,400. He belongs to the Dairies Association and thus automatically to the Federation of Swedish Farmers' Associations. The association takes delivery of the milk and mails him a check regularly on the thirteenth day of the month.

Last year, an average year, Pettersson sold three calves at $200 apiece. He delivered them to the Meat Marketing Association, which paid him the fixed price. He delivered his potatoes to the Purchasing and Selling Association, which paid him the regular price of $300 for his four-acre output.

What is more, Pettersson owns a tractor, and he drives it for other neighboring farmers for a fee. Eight farmers of the area have joined to buy a bull which they share. There is close co-operation between the farmers, with the exception of the Communist, who is an outcast in the community. Politically, Pettersson belongs to the Farmers' Party and is head of the local branch.

Pettersson estimates his gross annual income from the farm at $6,000, but there are many expenses for upkeep and repairs. Most of these are tax deductible. Such deductions are legitimate, and many farmers take advantage of them to evade taxation. Pettersson figures that his net income from the farm is approximately $1,600 a year, and that is what he, his wife, and daughter have to live on. It is sufficient to afford them a fair living, an occasional trip to the city, and nurse's training for the daughter as a sideline.

The Petterssons also cultivate a patch of flax which supplies mother and daughter with material for weaving during the winter months. Pettersson then turns his attention to his forestland. He sells the timber standing but does the carting. He does not belong to the Forestry Association because he can get a better price on his own. Pettersson is critical of the Forestry Association for its failure to obtain a higher price for his timber, but he states unequivocally that the farmers' co-operatives are indispensable. "We could never get along if we were not organized," he says. "We must work closely together politically, economically, and from the point of view of labor. That is our only salvation."

All farmers are not as comfortably fixed as the Petterssons. There is, for instance, the case of farmer Gunnar Ortman of Elfsby, east of Stockholm, whose small farm I visited. He owns eighteen acres of farmland, forty acres of woodland, six cows, and two horses. He grows hay and oats to feed the cattle and has a patch of potatoes which he sells. The woodland is not yet developed to the point where the timber can be cut. The farm provides only a meager living for him, his wife, and a sickly daughter who is unable to help on the farm. Ortman cannot afford to pay a helper and is obliged to employ a semi-demented youth provided by a mental institution in exchange for board and lodging. This is a painful situation for the family.

Ortman belongs to all the co-operative organizations from which he can derive any benefit: the Dairies Association, which picks up and markets the milk; the Meat Marketing Association, which slaughters his cattle; the Purchasing and Selling Association, which disposes of his potatoes; the Forestry Association, which will someday market his timber; and the Farmers' Union. But Ortman is struggling against circumstances which are relentlessly forcing him and many other small farmers out of business. The co-operatives enable him to carry on but they cannot save him.

The farmers' co-operatives have the strong support of the Farmers' Party, a minority in the present coalition government with the Social Democrats. The party holds 25 of 150 seats in the first chamber of Parliament and 26 seats in the second chamber out of 230—altogether 13 per cent of the seats in the legislature. The party has had a government of its own for a brief period, has participated previously in a number of coalitions, and has been a political force to reckon with, principally as a balance of power between the major parties.

The Farmers' Party proclaims itself to be the party of the middle way. It condemns "socialism which seeks security but overlooks freedom." It stands for private ownership and free enterprise and wants to preserve the soil for the farmers. It is for prohibition, stronger unions, increased social insurance, preventive care, relaxation of State control, decentralization of industries, and an international policy for "peace and freedom" which is isolationist.

The party head is Gunnar Hedlund, Minister of the Interior in the present government. He himself was a farmer who made his way by providing himself with a thorough education coupled with a shrewd business sense and a keen political acumen. Hedlund was raised in poverty on his father's twenty-acre farm in the northern woodlands. He later inherited the farm and also married the daughter of a wealthy neighboring farmer. The Hedlunds now own fifty acres of farmland and over 1,000 acres of woodland. Hedlund's failure to declare some of the profit of this forestland in a recent tax report led to charges of tax evasion. The Supreme Court found him guilty of making a false report but declared it was unintentional and he was let off with a fine. This incident became a major political issue, but he was nonetheless re-elected the party head and retains his seat in the cabinet.

Hedlund's early life was that of a struggling youth who worked hard to acquire an education, helping intermittently on the farm. He continued his studies until he obtained the coveted degree of Doctor of Laws from Uppsala University. Several minor political posts led him eventually to run for election to the second chamber of Parliament, where he has held a seat for the past fourteen years. He has been the party head since 1948.

Now in his fifties, Hedlund is a man of boundless energy.

Besides his duties as cabinet minister, he attends party meetings, travels about the country speaking to farming communities, and presides over meetings of the Forestry Association, his favorite sideline. The only way he can get any rest, he says, is to leave the country. And the last time he traveled abroad was to attend a meeting of the Council of Europe to which he was a delegate.

Hedlund's main objective, and that of his party and of all agricultural and co-operative groups, is to raise the standard of living of the farmer to equal that of the other labor groups. The average Swedish farmer earns from 15 to 20 per cent less than the lowest-paid industrial worker—the textile worker. Hedlund believes that the only answer is amalgamation of the smaller farms and increased mechanization. This means that the trend underway since the turn of the century which has accounted for a reduction in the farming population from three million to two million must continue at the sacrifice of the smaller farmer. The only alternative for the smaller farmer, as Hedlund sees it, is to cultivate vegetable-oil plant or acquire more timberland. The cultivation of rapeseed was introduced during the last war when Sweden, critically short of fats, imported vegetable-oil seed from Germany, used to produce margarine. This is a most profitable crop, but many farmers have not yet learned to grow it.

There is no disagreement in Sweden about the value of the farmers' co-operatives. It is recognized that they have become the backbone of the rural economy and are destined to play an increasing role as the process of farm rationalization continues. But the consumers' co-operatives are a topic of considerable controversy and are severely criticized by businessmen who support free enterprise.

The leaders of the consumers' co-operative movement can feel justly proud of the results they have achieved. The development of the movement has far exceeded their expectations, although they realize that it cannot continue to gain at the same rate. There is still room for more stores, but the saturation point cannot be far off. More particularly, there is an unlimited opportunity for expansion in industry which co-operative leaders feel has only begun to be tapped. KF has attained the remarkable position it now holds although controlling less than 2 per cent of Sweden's total industrial output. It has struck at the big business cartels, choosing its targets where the consumers had most to gain.

But KF's advance into industry has raised a difficult ideological problem. KF itself now threatens to become a vast monopoly, whereas combating monopoly has been one of the co-operative movement's main objectives. Co-operative leaders argue that since they do not aim to take over any one line of business completely, there is no question of establishing a monopoly. They contend, as Mauritz Bonow does, that the co-operatives would not misuse a monopolistic position because they keep prices down and because the shares are held by the consumers. But big business answers that if KF succeeds in undermining the business structure on an ever widening scale, private enterprise may perish. Business leaders point out furthermore that the co-operative movement is based on the principle of profit-sharing, but that one-third of all KF sales go to the Government or to clients outside of the co-operatives who do not therefore receive dividends. Although income is set aside for expansion, business leaders claim it is a violation of principle.

But when this has been said, the vast majority of the Swedish people admit that the co-operatives have performed a useful service by lowering the price level of many important consumer goods, thereby raising the standard of living for the masses. Co-operative stores have set a high standard which has compelled others to follow suit. Even businessmen, who are hardest hit, are ready to concede that the co-operatives have benefited the country. Kurt Soderberg, Vice President of the Association of Swedish Industries, which represents 3,000 business enterprises, told me, "KF should be given credit for what it has accomplished. No one in private business will deny that KF has been successful, particularly in rationalization and distribution. It has set an example for private retailers and forced them to raise their standard to meet the competition from KF. But private industry has unwittingly helped KF to expand by meeting the lower prices because it has been in no position to resist its growth."

Swedish private business has been losing ground to the co-operatives but has failed to provide any opposing program of its own. Businessmen complain of the inroads made by the co-operatives but they have been complacent. Some of this indifference is due to the general prosperity in the postwar years, which has provided business firms with more orders than they can fill. As long as this condition prevails, the average businessman need not worry about competition. This attitude has, to a large extent, assisted in KF's development.

The co-operative movement is of course popular among the masses, who benefit from low prices, but there is still a good deal of opposition among the upper classes, to the point of boycotting co-operative stores. Many of the socially elite would not be seen in a co-operative store as a matter of pride, although this prejudice is diminishing, while others remain aloof out of conviction, feeling they would be hammering another nail in the coffin of private enterprise. There is also a practical reason for the upper classes to abstain from shopping in co-operative stores since they do not deal in luxuries.

A prominent Swedish businessman who makes frequent trips abroad made this typical remark to me, "When I am abroad," he said, "I boast about the co-operatives as a true

Swede, but when I am back in Sweden I would not set my foot in a co-operative store or enterprise."

Charges are frequently made by Swedish businessmen that the co-operatives are favored by the Government. There have been many reports that private enterprises have been forced out of business by the co-operatives. I have attempted to investigate such charges, but I have been unable to discover a single instance in which this has occurred. Obviously, KF's price-cutting policy has undermined many businesses and has narrowed their margin of profit, but there is no evidence to show that this pressure has been applied in a corrupt manner. Neither the Association of Swedish Industries nor the Federation of Private Retailers to which I turned for examples of possible collusion could furnish any concrete proof that the co-operatives have benefited from Government support, aside from lower taxation.

There is evidence, however, to support charges that local town and village councils on which the Social Democrats are a majority have on occasion used their influence to grant better locations to co-operative stores, withheld building permits from private stores, and favored the co-operative stores in placing orders. Such complaints have been made openly in the Swedish Parliament. These instances no doubt occur because Social Democrats constitute the bulk of co-operative membership, but they are also a matter of political patronage. The fact is that the Government and the co-operatives are both organs of the labor movement.

CHAPTER VI

The Housing Problem

SWEDEN has set an example in modern housing for low income groups which provides a high standard for the people. There are no slums, and even the poorer and older housing, marked for destruction, has nothing in common with slums. The new housing provides all modern conveniences and is co-ordinated with planning schemes which emphasize landscaping, light, airiness, simplicity of style, and ever-changing originality of design.

The stress in building is on adaptation to surroundings so as to take advantage of nature. New buildings, both apartment houses and private homes, are carefully planned to fit in with the background. All windows are turned to the light, with open vistas wherever possible. The larger buildings are often of the box variety built with geometrical precision, with balconies for every apartment, but there are interesting variations. There are the "point" houses which rise like towers to a height of twelve to fourteen storys, with all apartments occupying corner space, and the "star" houses—a set of three apartments with a central stairway. These are joined to form hexagonal courtyards and are located at such an angle that it is impossible to look into the neighbor's apartment because of reflection. There are enclosed gardens, courtyards, and terraces everywhere, with a profusion of flowers. The Swedish people are particularly fond of flowers and color, as if to seek relief from the monotony of the long, dark winter months. Every attempt is made to provide a bright and cheerful atmosphere both by means of the plain, clearcut architectural style and the furnishings. Sweden is able, in this respect, to make good use of many of its own home products such as glass, ceramics, textiles, and light wood furniture.

But this progressive trend does not mean that the Swedish people are well housed. There is an acute housing shortage in Sweden, as almost everywhere else in Europe, and there is serious overcrowding. A recent Government survey revealed that an estimated 30 per cent of the population is living in overcrowded quarters, meaning less than one room for two persons; that 15 per cent of all dwellings are dilapidated and lack running water and sewer facilities in the cities, while the proportion in the country is as high as 66 per cent. There is a shortage of 70,000 dwelling units which the Government plans to overcome in ten years.

There are a number of reasons for the shortage. In the first place, it dates back to the turn of the century, when Sweden became industrialized. There was a consequent flow of labor from the farm to the cities, which have quadrupled their population. The housing situation was aggravated during the war years when Sweden, virtually blockaded, had to step up her home production and was also engaged in supplying some of the war needs for both sets of belligerents. Shortage of labor and building materials led to a drop in building, which fell off from the high point of 59,000 dwelling units in 1939 to 17,000 in 1941, with a gradual recovery to 58,000 in 1954.

The Government's housing budget for 1956 calls for the construction of 53,000 new units.

Overcrowding became worse as the result of a policy, initiated in the twenties, of concentrating on small apartments, consisting for the most part of only one room and kitchen. These small units accounted for half of all home building during the twenty-year period between the two world wars. While these apartments were conceived with minute attention to detail and a pride in efficiency, they provided cramped accommodation which reached a crisis when these one-room units, intended for single persons or couples, had to suffice for three or four persons. Swedish housing seems peculiarly to have skipped over a generation. It went from the large apartments of the nineties, with many oversized, high-ceilinged rooms, to the postage-stamp cubicles where everything has to be exactly in its right place. There was no halfway, and there are today few medium-sized dwellings in Sweden. This need is now being recognized, and it is the aim of the Government's housing policy to provide every family of two persons with a minimum of one room and an additional room for every two children. It is considered now that a family with two children should therefore have at least a two-room apartment with kitchen, and a family with three or four children should have a three-room apartment.

Conditions are such now that many young couples are unable to get married because they have no place to live together, and not infrequently they are obliged to double up in one room, with little prospect of finding a larger apartment when the first child arrives. Although the municipalities list applicants for apartments and give priority to couples with young children, the average waiting time for an apartment obtained in this manner is between five and seven years. This has, of course, led to a black market like that in most European countries since the war. The black-market rate for an apartment in Stockholm is about $1,000 a room.

The Government controls the building situation. By means of a double licensing system it decides who may build and where and when. One license is needed to build in conformity with the town planning and the other to obtain the labor and start the work. The Government also provides loans at extremely low rates, in some cases up to the full amount of the building cost, to municipalities, co-operatives, and to private individuals, particularly in the low-income groups. But this aid is furnished on definite conditions which require the recipient to conform to a general building plan and to meet certain building requirements with regard to size and standard.

Over 80 per cent of all dwelling units are built with Government assistance in the form of loans and subsidies. The Government first came to control the housing situation as an emergency wartime measure, but this has been maintained ever since by yearly extensions by Parliament. It became necessary during the war for the Government to allocate building materials which were in shortage and to direct labor into the channels where it was most needed. In the immediate postwar years, labor was diverted mainly to export industries to bolster Sweden's diminishing gold reserve. Now, with the financial situation improved, the Government continues its control for the double purpose of checking inflation and leveling out the supply of labor. These arguments in favor of continued Government control have been bitterly attacked by the political opposition parties, which contend that greater freedom in building would lower building costs and reduce the need for subsidies. The Government argument that it is able to even out the supply of labor is rejected by private building contractors, who claim that the Government's interference frequently deprives them of labor when it is most advantageous to build and renders planning extremely difficult and uneconomical.

The licensing system is handled by local labor agencies working in conjunction with the Housing Board. Applications for licenses must specify in detail not only what sort of a building is to be erected but must contain estimates of the cost and must comply with Government regulations regarding space and other architectural features. The actual construction is not undertaken by the Government, but is in the hands of private contractors.

There are two principal types of loans and subsidies, one applying to small houses for one or two families, and the other to apartment houses. In the case of the smaller homes, assistance is given to private individuals up to between 75 and 90 per cent of the estimated cost of the building, although the estimate generally falls short of the actual cost. There is a bank mortgage of 50 per cent of the building cost, a second mortgage—known as an "own-home" loan— of at least another 25 per cent and sometimes 40 per cent in cases where a subsidy is provided for low-income families, and there are deductions in amortization for poorer families with children. These include subsidies for children and for fuel for the family.

As for apartment houses, the Government grants a third mortgage as a subsidy. This is intended to keep rents down by reducing the cost of building. It is figured on the basis of space and varies in different localities according to the local building costs. There is a first mortgage of 60 per cent and a second mortgage of another 10 per cent; the third mortgage is reckoned at 30 per cent for community projects— which thus receive a loan up to the full building cost—25 per cent for co-operative enterprises, and 15 per cent for private companies or individuals. The interest on all mortgages and loans is only 3 per cent. In addition, there are special loans for repairs, including substantial subsidies for poorer families.

The granting of building licenses is decided arbitrarily by the housing authorities. If there is a definite policy, it is not stated in the law nor is it clearly apparent. There are persons who have been waiting for permits for years, while others seem to obtain them readily. A high official of the Housing Board told me that the Government's policy is to allow as much building as possible with the available supply of labor. There was a time when there was a scarcity of building materials, but that has been largely overcome, and while there is full employment in Sweden, the labor market is not as restricted as it was formerly. If any policy can be discerned, it is that low-income groups, particularly families with children, are favored first. Also, some priority seems to be given to those who are willing to build their homes themselves. There is a class of semiprofessional workmen who are willing to put in their own time and effort in building their homes, often with the help of neighbors, and they are most liable to receive Government encouragement. If the lower income groups happen to be Social Democrats, that is because most laborers, members of trade unions, belong to the Social Democratic Party. As for apartments, the Government admittedly gives a priority to municipal building and to the co-operatives over private enterprise.

Arthur Andersson provides an example of a workman who built his own home with the help of neighbors and with maximum Government support. He and his wife and two young daughters lived formerly in a comfortable modern three-room apartment in a Stockholm suburb and were therefore not in need of housing, as are hundreds of thousands of others, but Andersson had no trouble in obtaining the necessary licenses, presumably because he wished to do as much of the building himself as possible and because he belonged in the lower income category to which first consideration is given.

The new Andersson home would do justice to any residential area in the United States. It is a one-and-a-half-story house, built on a slope with two floors on one side and one on the other. It is built of lightweight cement and is an example of Swedish modern architecture of a common type at its best. A winding staircase leads up to the living room on the second floor at the rear of the house. It is an elongated rectangular room, about twenty by fourteen feet. It serves also as dining room. There are large windows which give it the effect of a glassed-in veranda. There is an odd fireplace which projects into the room in a cone shape. The furniture is plain, but there is a freshness in the tints of the wallpaper and the newness of the home which imparts a cheerful atmosphere. There are four small bedrooms, a large kitchen with all modern conveniences, and a garage in the basement. The Anderssons are obviously proud of their home, and this is easily understandable since Andersson himself put in 1,800 hours of work in its construction.

Andersson, who is a foreman in a carpenter's shop, drew up his own plans for the house with the help of a neighbor, a building engineer. He submitted the plans and an estimate of the building cost to the local housing authorities and obtained the needed licenses six months later, authorizing him to start building at once. The construction was carried out by Andersson with the assistance of three neighbors: the building engineer, a bricklayer, and a painter, all of whom have built their own homes in a similar manner, and with occasional hired help. The piping and electrical fixtures, however, were installed by regular firms as required by law. The construction required two years, and there is nothing about the finished product which would in any way indicate that it is an amateur undertaking. On the contrary, the detailed workmanship conveys the impression that more than the usual care has gone into it.

The original estimated value of the house when the building permits were sought was $11,000, but when it was completed it was revalued at $14,000 and refinanced. Andersson obtained a maximum loan of 90 per cent of the estimated cost of construction, and the home was financed as follows:

Total estimated building cost	$14,000	100 per cent
Bank mortgage	7,000	50 per cent
State own-home loan	5,600	40 per cent
(incl. subsidy free from		
tax and amortization)	(1,600)	
Owner's share	1,400	10 per cent

It actually cost Andersson $15,000 to build the house, so that his own outlay was $2,400. Housing authorities always value the house below cost in order to prevail upon the people to exercise the utmost economy in building. Any expenses in excess of the estimate are the builder's, and while it is theoretically possible to build within the limits of the estimate, in practice the outlay is generally between 15 and 20 per cent. There are definite limits with regard to luxuries, but it is a requisite that homes, if they are to be financed with State support, must be equipped with central heating, running water, and bath.

Andersson's annual payments on his house are small and total only $570, or $47.50 a month. His payments are:

Interest at 3 per cent on $7,000 mortgage	$210
Interest at 3 per cent on $4,000 State loan	
(excluding $1,600 subsidy)	120
Amortization of mortgage (indefinite)	80
Amortization of State loan over 25 years	160
	$570

First co-operative store operated in Sweden, now a museum, and below, a modern countryside *konsum* building.

Albin Johansson, Chairman of the Board of the Swedish consumers co-operatives, standing before co-operative headquarters in Stockholm.

Iron ore mines at Kiruna, in northern Lapland, working under floodlights during the dark winter months. Below, the Luma lamp factory, operated by Swedish co-operatives.

Typical small Swedish farm.

Apartment house unit operated by the Swedish welfare system, and, below, Swedish worker Adolf Ginsberg and his family, who live in the building.

Vällingby, a modern suburban welfare community near Stockholm, housing 75,000 people and maintained jointly by the municipality and the co-operative system.

Southern Hospital in Stockholm, with 600 rooms and 1,200 beds. Built at a cost of $7,000,000, it is the largest in Scandinavia.

King Gustav VI Adolph of Sweden, with his grandson, Crown Prince Carl Gustav.

The State own-home loan is amortized over twenty-five years, but there is no set time for paying off the bank loan, which is generally fixed at a flat rate of about $80 a year. The Andersson loan would be amortized over a period of approximately eighty-eight years. The banks are extremely lenient with regard to the terms for repayment of building loans, which are considered to be among the safest investments.

Andersson estimates his own work in building his home to be worth approximately $1,500, figured on the basis of his earning capacity as a carpenter. His income is not in the low category which would entitle him to special subsidies for his children and for heating, which would have further reduced his costs. Andersson has already been offered $22,000 for his house, but he has no intention of selling it. He is allowed to, but then he would be unable to obtain permits to build another home. This is a way of preventing speculation in building.

Two-thirds of the population in Sweden live in apartment houses. In Stockholm and other big cities there are a number of "collective" houses. The term is inaccurate, since there is no joint ownership or operation of the houses, but there are household conveniences which are shared by the tenants.

The best known of these houses is Marieberg in Stockholm, one of the first of its kind built experimentally a decade ago and intended mainly for young married couples with children to raise. The special features of this house are a nursery, operated by skilled personnel, where the tenants may leave their children for the day when they go to work; a recreation room for older children when they return from school; maid service; a laundry; and a low-priced restaurant with meals by subscription. The tenants are compelled to subscribe to a minimum of twenty-five dinners a month. Many of them object to this and would prefer to cook their own meals. The apartments are small and consist of from one to three rooms and kitchen.

Mr. and Mrs. Bo Josephson are a typical couple among the tenants of Marieberg. He is a young engineer who was employed in building the new American Embassy in Stockholm. Mrs. Josephson works in a store. They have two young boys, seven and three years old. The Josephsons moved in just after the house was built, when they were newly married and thought that a two-room apartment would suffice for their needs. Ever since the children were born, they have been trying to obtain a larger apartment, but without result. All four of them, parents and children, live in one small bedroom, while the other room serves as living room and dining room. There is a small kitchen which they use for cooking breakfast and lunch over the weekends. At night they eat in the restaurant, where they get a plain forty-cent dinner. Children's meals are half price. The meals are cheap but monotonous, since it is a set menu and there is no choice of food.

Both Mr. and Mrs. Josephson leave for work at eight o'clock in the morning and deposit the children in the nursery, where they are looked after with some sixty other children of tenants. The cost is one dollar per child a day and it includes lunch and an afternoon snack. The only drawback is that the nursery will not take care of sick children, so that Mrs. Josephson has to stay home if one of the children is ill. The Josephsons are grateful for the maid service which they pay for by the hour and for the laundry.

Mr. and Mrs. Hilding Amlin, other tenants who are in a higher income bracket, are not as satisfied as the Josephsons. He is an engineer with the Ericsson Telephone Company and she is a top-level worker in the Ministry of Social Welfare. Together they probably earn $5,000 to $6,000 a year. They also have two children, both girls. But the children are older, nine and five, and the Amlins are not at all sure that the institutionalized bringing-up is the right one. They feel that a day nursery is not the proper place for a child of five. The elder girl goes to school and is also looked after by a trained professional when she comes home before the parents return from work. But the Amlins admit that the collective house has many advantages. It is cheap, there is no need to shop for food except the bare necessities for breakfast, they are always sure of service, and the children are cared for when the parents are away. In fact, the nursery provides baby sitters at night for a small fee.

There is nothing collective about the relationship of the tenants. For the most part, they do not know each other. There is a characteristic Swedish aloofness among the tenants, who have no more than a nodding acquaintance and do not desire to go beyond that. The feeling is that a man's home is his castle, and neighbors are generally indifferent unless there is some personal or family tie.

Of all the welfare projects in Sweden, one of the best advertised, if only by its dominant position, is *Kvinnohuset*—the House for Women—built on a high cliff overlooking the city of Stockholm. It is a fourteen-story building, a skyscraper by Swedish standards, which rises high over the neighboring rooftops. It is in the center facing a long, wide thoroughfare and is a landmark that can be seen from almost any part of the city. The great incoming and outgoing continental airliners seem to slip by the side of its tower rather than to pass over it.

The house is intended for single working women. No married women are admitted as tenants and no children. If a tenant gets married or becomes a mother, she must move. A well-known chocolate firm, whose label is a stork, once proposed to install a neon sign on the building to advertise its product, but the women of the house protested that a stork would be a most inappropriate emblem. Men are admitted to the house as guests but may not live there. Mrs. Olga Johansson, the caretaker of the Women's House and, in effect, its guardian, has a strange philosophy. She believes that it is better for women to live there and receive their men friends than to get married and have no decent place to live in because of the housing shortage.

The house was built to provide low-cost living for single working women who, it was felt, were being overlooked by the State in its concern for the welfare of families. But the experiment has not proved a success and the house has attained a somewhat unenviable repuation, mainly because of a current bestseller entitled *The House for Women* by the novelist Ulla Isaksson, who claims, however, that she was never in it and that any resemblance is purely coincidental. But her statement has convinced few people, since her description of the Tower House, as she calls it, so closely resembles the original. Reviewers called it a masterpiece in reporting. And when movie men tried to force their way in to provide a realistic background for the filming of the novel, they were turned away by Mrs. Johansson with the comment that the tenants were serious women who had "no time for sex and such nonsense." She was upheld by the four women members of the board, with the only male member dissenting.

The novel lends far more glamour and drama to the house than the casual visitor will find. It is a triangle love story involving two women tenants, culminating in a murder, and as a sideline the daughter of the janitor jumps off the roof when she finds she is pregnant and cannot go on living in the house.

In reality the House for Women seems forbidding and dreary. It was originally intended for young and lonely working women with low incomes, but the limits on age and income have both been raised since. The tenants are now mostly middle-aged women. They include nurses, office workers, and shop assistants. The rents are extremely low. A single room with washroom and kitchen rents for only $115 a year, and the rent for a two-room apartment, which should be shared by two women, is $211 a year. The rooms are scarcely larger than cubicles, but the tenants seem to fit in with the same neatness and precision that is to be found all over Sweden.

After operating the house for eight years, Mrs. Johansson, herself a widow, believes that the experiment provides no pattern for the future, and the municipality which built it and subsidizes its operation has come to the same conclusion.

Co-operative housing now accounts for approximately 20 per cent of all new building in Sweden and is expected to reach 25 per cent within the next few years, with the Government strongly supporting the co-operatives. The main co-operative organization is known as HSB, the Swedish initials for the National Association of Tenants' Savings and Building Societies. The association participates with the municipalities in town planning, supplies its own architects, and provides some of the building materials, but leaves the construction in the hands of private contractors.

The housing co-operatives do not aim to provide lower cost housing, but co-operative management among tenants is designed to bring about cheaper operation of apartment buildings. All co-operative building receives support to the extent of 95 per cent of construction costs.

Tenants buy a share in HSB for ten dollars. This constitutes their membership. They then make a deposit of from 5 to 10 per cent of the proportionate building cost of their apartment. When the tenants have moved in, they form a co-operative association of their own to administer the building. The rent includes operation costs, amortization of the loans, and a contribution toward a fund for repairs. Tenants may sell their share for the amount of the payments made on the property but may not make a profit on the transaction.

Co-operative housing advertisements stress that "Your rent goes to pay for your own home." HSB puts it this way: "Over 55,000 families all over the country, members of HSB, own their own homes. The rent, figured at actual cost, is paid to themselves. The initial payment and part of the rent goes toward amortization. It is, to a large extent, money saved. HSB can be called a savings bank in which the members, over the years, have invested 160,000,000 crowns ($32,-000,000)."

HBS officials point out that the greatest advantage for tenants of co-operative apartments is that the administration is in their own hands, so that they have a special interest in proper upkeep and in economical operation. Whatever HSB saves by supplying building materials at low cost from factories operated by the consumers' co-operatives, such as lumber, bricks, marble, plumbing and sanitary equipment, it spends on landscaping and gardening.

Aside from apartments, HSB turns out prefabricated houses in its own factories. They are built and financed with Government help up to 90 per cent of the cost, while the remaining 10 per cent, the owner's share of the investment, is represented by his own labor in assembling the home. Such homes are frequently erected with members of the family and friends or neighbors participating in the construction work. But they are not particularly cheap. A four-room house, equipped with modern plumbing and electricity, will cost as much as $10,000, including the land. Swedish factories are now turning out about 25,000 prefabricated houses a year, of which half are exported.

A preview of future Swedish housing may be seen in several community developments in the neighborhood of Stockholm. Among these is Vällingby, a new suburb of 75,000 inhabitants. It is a combined municipal and co-operative enterprise, with the municipality responsible for two-thirds of the building and the co-operatives, one-third. The original idea was to create a self-sufficient community where the inhabitants could work, shop, and live without ever having to go elsewhere. It was to center around local industries which were to be enticed to settle there by readily granted building permits and cheap land. But the municipality failed to attract the industries and the town has turned out to be just another community center, patterned on the suburban areas adjoining the larger cities in the United States. A priority is given to local workers in living quarters, but they are mostly shopkeepers.

Vällingby does, however, indicate the trend, which is to give the municipalities and the co-operatives an increasing role in the development of housing with Government support at the sacrifice of private ownership.

It is against State control and regulation of the building industry that Olle Engkvist, Sweden's leading contractor, raises a voice of protest. No story of modern Swedish building would be complete without mention of his name. He built Government House and the Concert Hall in Stockholm, renovated Parliament, and built the City Hall in Gothenburg. He is also the originator of many of the most up-to-date housing projects and apartment houses, and his firm built the new $1,500,000 American Embassy in Stockholm.

Engkvist rose by his own efforts from bricklayer and retains a love for his early trade, which he says has undergone little technical change since the days of the Egyptian Pharaohs. He has three brothers working for him. Two of them are bricklayers and the other is a painter.

As a member of the bricklayers' union in his early days, Engkvist was a Social Democrat but, commensurate with his rise, he has swung over politically from left to right and is now rated a Conservative and a bitter opponent of Government regimentation. He marked the thirtieth anniversary of his association with the building trade by abandoning control of his business and turning it over to his coworkers. He wrote them, "I feel that my task is ended. Certainly there are still many tempting projects, but under present conditions with all the existing rules and regulations, I cannot carry out the work I had planned. The spirit of the age, which no longer tolerates free private enterprise, is crushing initiative. The 'New Deal' in Sweden represents a mentality without initiative and therefore without pleasure in work. The individual is supposed merely to await his share of the work and no longer has the opportunity to enjoy the thrill that springs from bold ideas and objectives. Those who, like myself, had vision must now reconcile themselves to a procedural mentality."

And as if in protest against the modernism that he helped to create, Engkvist has retired to an eighteenth-century mansion which has nothing in common with the precision buildings he has erected for so many others.

CHAPTER VII

Compulsory Health Insurance

IN SWEDEN co-operation in combating disease had its roots a thousand years ago. Then the elders of every town and village were the custodians of what was known as a "stave of mercy." This was a square wooden stick, about three feet long, and was handed to a family as an emblem of duty. The family took upon itself to assist any sick or needy person and, once this service was performed, put its stamp on the stick and passed it on to another family.

With the stave of mercy went this legend: "Good neighbor. The stave of mercy passes on to Thee; sit by the bedside of Thy friend; fill to the brim the cup of health, giving hope and courage." But it was not merely a matter of sitting by the bedside of a sick patient. The duties were many. It might be the task of plowing a neighbor's field, or caring for his cattle, or baking for his wife, or it might be a matter of financial help. This practice endured in Sweden for three centuries.

In the Middle Ages a first effort was made to raise public funds for the care of the sick and the poor. It is surprising to learn that in those days a small amount was deducted from the pay of every worker and placed in a community chest—an early forerunner of pay-check deductions. The money was used whenever the community judged it was needed. Many of these old wooden chests with a large coin slot in the lid are preserved to this day in Sweden.

Swedes claim that, like the Romans, they were among the first people to take baths, but that this custom disappeared in the Middle Ages under foreign influence. Swedish doctors have little good to say for the foreign institutions which gave their country the first semblance of medical care. Catholic convents provided some measure of care for the sick and needy, but whatever was accomplished was wiped out by a single stroke when King Gustav Vasa banned Catholicism from Sweden in the early sixteenth century. The ban was partially revoked in the latter part of the eighteenth century, but it was not until 1951 that Catholic churches were given the same rights as the Swedish church and that convents were allowed to return.

After the Catholics were driven out, there was a dark period when the sick went virtually without care; but the need to segregate lepers, of which there were thousands at the time, led to the gradual establishment of leper colonies. They were located on small islands in the countless lakes of Sweden, particularly in the southern part of the country. There are now three cases of leprosy in Sweden, all under close medical surveillance.

Early medical care in Sweden was undertaken by barbers, bath attendants, midwives, and by a limited number of foreign doctors who were admitted by royal decree. The barbers came to be known as "barber surgeons," and the Barbers' Guild became in time the first surgical society and took its place along with the Medical Society.

Toward the end of the eighteenth century, a Government

ordinance required every province to provide a general hospital and an insane asylum. Now there are at least one or two central hospitals in every province which provide hospitalization for an average county population of 200,000 persons. The aim of the Medical Board is to double the number of these hospitals. This figure does not include special hospitals which handle epidemics and care for maternity patients and the chronically and mentally ill. Altogether there are close to 800 hospitals in Sweden, with room for 80,000 patients.

Largely as the result of the vast expenditure by the Government and the municipalities for medical care, Sweden now enjoys a life expectancy which ranks third in the world and is surpassed only by Norway and the Netherlands. The life expectancy for Swedish women is 71.6 years of age and for men, 69. This is despite the fact that Sweden's climate is not a particularly healthy one, with long winters, a minimum of sunshine, and generally rigorous conditions. An era of prosperity, bringing with it a high standard of living, has contributed to the relatively good health conditions within the country.

Ever since it came to power, the Social Democratic Party had promised compulsory health insurance, but it was bitterly opposed by the doctors. The Government was compelled to move slowly because of the tremendous cost involved, which became the more apparent from the British example.

As a first step toward compulsory health insurance, a special Social Care Committee was appointed in 1937. It took seven years for this committee to formulate its report, which proposed a scheme of cash benefits during illness based on income. But the Government then felt the principle was undemocratic and that all beneficiaries should be entitled to the same compensation, in line with the British Beveridge Plan. Difficulty was also encountered in merging the proposed health insurance with the existing employment accident insurance. The plan was revised to accord with Government policy and somewhat reluctantly approved by Parliament in 1946, but its enforcement was repeatedly postponed, principally because the Government feared the expense.

While the Social Care Committee was occupied mainly with the technical and financial aspects of the new scheme, the Government appointed another commission to look into the medical side. This commission, headed by Dr. Axel Höjer, then chairman of the Medical Board, made an exhaustive five-year study. Its 800-page report went much further than the Government had ever anticipated and made a series of recommendations which included placing all doctors on a straight salary basis.

The keynote of the controversial Höjer Report was to be found in a single sentence which read, "All medical care should be available to anyone in need of it with no expense at the time it is needed." There was no objection to this principle, but the program was considered to be unrealistic. It was characteristic of the vague idealism of its chairman that it had been worked out without any precise estimate of the cost involved.

The Höjer Report paralleled the report of the Social Care Committee in recommending free hospital care and a refund of three-quarters of outpatients' medical expenses. But it went beyond this and suggested, as a long-term objective, that outpatients should eventually be treated free of charge, so that all medical care would become free. It placed emphasis on what it called "preventive" medicine and proposed that all Swedish citizens should be medically examined twice a year. This idea was rejected by the Medical Association, which figured that any effective examination would consume an hour's time and that even if every Swede were examined only once a year, more doctors would be required for that purpose alone than exist in the country. But the most controversial feature of the Höjer Report was the recommendation that doctors be placed on a salary basis and that private fees be abolished.

The Höjer Report was circulated, according to Swedish parliamentary procedure, to over a hundred different organizations and groups concerned and was opposed by most of them. The Medical Association declared bluntly that "it offered stones instead of bread." It countered with a slogan of its own calling for "the best possible care for anyone in need of it without economic hardship." The association categorically opposed the idea of a salary for doctors without fees. It felt the Government-paid doctors would result in uniformity of treatment, destroy private initiative, and lower the medical standard.

LO, the Confederation of Trade Unions, declared itself in complete agreement with the principle that "all citizens should be guaranteed free medical care by the community—a right which is as natural in a progressive society as the right of education irrespective of the individual's means." The Employers' Federation, on the other hand, called it "complete socialization of the medical profession."

As a result of the criticism directed against it, the Höjer Report was set aside. Its author became so unpopular among medical men that he was forced to relinquish the position as head of the Medical Board which he had held for eighteen years and seek refuge as a missionary in India, far away from the scene of controversy at home.

In 1952, the Government appointed a third commission, known as the Social Insurance Investigating Committee, to draw up a new program for compulsory health insurance which would be less expensive for the State and which would co-ordinate health and accident insurance. After a ten-month study, the committee came forward with a series of proposals which included a new health insurance program, a new maternity bill, a plan to bring accident insurance within the scope of the medical program, a bill to provide free medicine for critical ailments, and a tax scheme to finance the various reforms. All of these proposals together constitute the basis of the new compulsory health insurance.

The new legislation was approved by Parliament with only slight opposition from the Conservative minority and came into effect on January 1, 1955. While the Social Democratic Party has taken credit for most of the welfare projects, the other parties have generally gone along with them and have even competed in claiming authorship. The new compulsory health insurance replaced a voluntary Government-subsidized insurance, covering 60 per cent of the population, which provided very low cost hospitalization and a refund of two-thirds of medical expenses.

The new system falls into two parts. Every Swedish citizen is insured and entitled to free hospitalization and a refund of three-quarters of his medical expenses at public clinics or outside of hospitals. On the other hand, every wage earner with an income of $240 a year or more receives a daily allowance based on his income when absent from work on account of illness.

The free hospital care is limited to two years for the same disease but may be continued if the patient develops some other disease or complications. If he is not cured at the end of the two-year period, he may receive an invalid's pension. For old people who are already pensioned, the free hospitalization is limited to three months; after that, they can be cared for in a home for the aged where medical attention is provided free.

By far the most expensive item is the cash benefit paid to sick persons while absent from work. This varies between 60 cents a day for a person earning between $240 and $360 a year to $4.00 a day for a person in the highest category, earning $2,800 or more a year. Those earning more than this maximum figure may supplement their benefit by privately insuring themselves for an additional amount. After three months' illness, the per diem rate is reduced, and varies between 60 cents and $2.40 a day. A wife is automatically insured at the lowest rate unless she is herself a wage earner, and children under sixteen receive the free hospital and medical care.

Actually, the compulsory health insurance is not free, although the people are not too conscious of the cost. An insurance premium is included in income-tax returns and varies between $4.60 and $30 a year, according to income. Those whose income falls below $240 a year are insured free, while persons who are not wage earners pay the minimum fee and receive free hospitalization and the medical refund but no cash subsidy.

Rolf Broberg, secretary of the committee which drafted the new laws, says the cash benefits were fixed to compensate wage earners for about half of their income. The committee felt that to pay more would be to encourage people to stay away from work unnecessarily. Broberg explains that the committee calculated on an average of seventeen days absence from work annually. This was a guess, since there was no way of telling to what extent people would take advantage of the new benefits.

Accident insurance fits into the framework of the health insurance. A worker injured in the course of his occupation is entitled to the regular benefits of the health insurance for the first three months of sickness or incapacity, after which the accident insurance benefits come into force and provide invalidity pensions up to a maximum of $2,020 a year for complete incapacity. Most workers are collectively insured either by their unions or in groups to cover the period beyond the three months provided by the compulsory health insurance.

A new maternity bill grants a cash benefit of $54 to each new mother and of $80 if there are twins or more. The woman obtains free transportation to and from hospital at the time of childbirth, free hospitalization and delivery, and is entitled to the same daily cash benefit as if she were ill up to a maximum of ninety days.

Medicines prescribed by a physician are free for certain critical diseases and the charge is half for all other prescriptions above an initial sixty cents. Pharmacies are reimbursed by the Government insurance agency. Eyeglasses and false teeth are not included free nor at reduced prices, but artificial limbs are free in certain cases under the accident insurance law.

The Swedish system allows both doctors and patients much greater freedom than the British. Whereas in England a patient has no choice of doctor but is included in a panel of patients, a Swede may choose his own hospital, provided it is within the municipality where he pays his taxes, and may select what hospital clinic he will visit, or call on any private doctor of his own choice and still be entitled to the medical refund.

This requires further explanation. Except for emergency ambulance cases when patients are delivered to the nearest hospital, a Swede may choose his hospital provided there is room. This usually entails a period of waiting, but if there is no great urgency, he will wait his turn. Once in hospital, however, he must accept whatever medical or surgical care is available unless he is a private patient. If he is an outpatient, he may be treated at any hospital clinic or he may go from one to another, but again he must accept the service of the doctor who happens to be on duty. Outside of hospitals, he is free to visit any doctor he pleases, with the reservation that he will receive a refund of three-quarters of his medical expenses according to a fixed schedule of rates, although most doctors charge more, and he will have to pay the difference. Most specialists have little regard for the Medical Board's tariffs.

Close to 90 per cent of all doctors in Sweden are employed in some way by the Medical Board, the municipalities, or the county councils, but with the exception of junior doctors working in hospitals, most of them maintain their own private practice, which provides their main source of income. Swedish doctors are unanimously opposed to the British system of limiting doctors to a Government fee.

The other essential difference between the British and Swedish systems concerns cash benefits during sickness. The British system provides a uniform rate, whereas the Swedish plan is based on income. This has been a hotly debated subject in Sweden for years between those who considered the flat rate the more democratic way and those who felt that the cash benefit should compensate a wage earner for his loss of income during illness and help him maintain his customary standard of living. The argument was settled in favor of the wage basis mainly because it was found to be much cheaper for the Government, since it is able to collect higher insurance rates. Under the flat rate, the Government would have had to pay approximately 75 per cent of the cost of the medical program instead of 29 per cent. It was also easier to coordinate the health insurance with the accident insurance, which was on the wage scale.

The free medical and surgical care applies to patients in a ward, a unit consisting generally of thirty beds, including four private rooms, four semiprivate rooms, and three or more larger rooms accommodating four to six patients in each. The allotment is dependent upon the condition of the patient and the space available at the time of admission. The more serious cases are assigned to private or semiprivate rooms whenever possible, and when the patients improve they are often moved into the larger rooms.

Patients who choose a private or semiprivate room are considered private patients and pay accordingly. There is, of course, a considerable difference in treatment between a private patient and one in the ward. The private patient receives far more personal attention. He may have a doctor of his own choice and a special nurse, while a patient in the ward will be looked after by whoever happens to be on duty, either an assistant doctor or an intern, unless the case is a particularly complicated one requiring a specialist, and he will have to share the nurse with the other patients. Private patients may also receive visitors freely, whereas visiting hours in the ward are limited to an hour or two a day. There is no difference in the food served in the hospitals.

The cost of a private or semiprivate room varies according to hospitals and may be anywhere from $2.50 to $5.00 for a semiprivate room and double that amount for a private one. But even these charges do not fully cover the cost of hospitalization, which is estimated at an average of over ten dollars a day for every hospital case. The difference is paid by the municipality or county council from taxes. There is a "voluntary" charge per day for private patients for surgical care, according to a scale fixed by the Medical Board, as follows:

	Semiprivate Room	Private Room
Complicated operation	$8 to $30	$15 to $60
Average operation	$6 to $20	$10 to $40
Minor operation	$4 to $ 6	$ 6 to $15

The patient can determine the fee within these limits, and there is an additional small charge for the medical care.

Medical expenses for outpatients at hospital clinics are

paid by the patient according to a fixed scale for various types of treatment, but three-quarters of the expenses are refunded. The charges for outpatient care were raised just before the new compulsory health insurance came into effect, with the result that patients who received a two-thirds refund under the former voluntary insurance system now pay about the same rate.

All hospitals in Sweden are crowded, and there are long waiting lists. This is not new, but existed under the former voluntary insurance system which provided very low cost hospitalization. The overcrowding may also be attributed to the housing shortage, leaving no extra room for a sick person; the shortage of servants, providing little extra help at home; and the fact that in many cases both husband and wife are employed and no one is at home to care for the sick member of the family.

Southern Hospital in Stockholm, so called because it is located in the southern and poorer section of the city, is a model for the rest of the country and is one of the best hospitals anywhere. It was built at a cost of $7,000,000 and took seventeen years to complete. It is a great rectangular eight-story building, a quarter-mile long, set high on a cliff overlooking the city. It is impressive because of its very simplicity as well as its size. All the 600 rooms face outside, and they are large, bright, and cheerful, with a view over the wooded slopes and inland waterways of the archipelago. There are spacious entrances on two levels, elevators for every section, and long, wide marble corridors—too long for the convenience of the nursing staff and personnel, who use scooters to get about.

The hospital extends far below ground in the granite rock to serve in the event of war. There is a large underground shelter which can accommodate 2,000 persons, and there are 700 beds, two operating rooms, and an X-ray department. A tunnel connects with a railway so that wounded can be carried to the operating tables directly from arriving trains. The hospital has its own well in case the main water supply should be cut off, its own power plant, and a radio station to contact the hospital staff and patients as well as for entertainment.

In building the hospital, every type of experiment was tried out by the late Hjalmar Cederström, the resourceful architect. An experimental ward was constructed and doctors, nurses, and patients were asked to give their opinions. For example, the four-patient room was decided upon because it was found that whenever a sick person moved out of a six-patient room, there was an immediate demand for the corner space. Now every patient has his corner.

Southern Hospital has 1,200 beds, with an extra 300 in a separate wing for convalescents. It takes care of 30,000 inpatients a year, while the clinic lists as many as 380,000 visits. Of course, this does not indicate the number of patients, since many return for treatment.

Medical care in municipal and county hospitals is of a high grade, but one of the most common complaints is that it is impersonal. This is largely due to the pressure on the medical and nursing staff and rules out the type of care to be found in the few remaining private institutions. Southern Hospital has only ninety-three beds in private or semiprivate rooms; this is typical of hospitals throughout Sweden, where the private wards account for less than 10 per cent of the patients. There is now a movement afoot to abolish private care in hospitals and reserve the private and semiprivate rooms for isolation purposes only.

With few exceptions, Swedish doctors are not accustomed to devoting the same personal attention to patients that Americans expect of their physicians. It frequently takes weeks for a patient to secure an appointment with a doctor, and few doctors make home calls except in cases of real emergency. The Swedish public, conscious of the burden on the medical profession, seems too readily to accept this condition as normal. This accounts for an added burden on the hospital clinics, which are always available for emergency treatment and where assistants and interns are on constant duty.

The administrator of the new health insurance plan is Dr. Arthur Engel, who succeeded Dr. Höjer as head of the Medical Board. Engel is alert, conscientious, businesslike, and well liked by the medical profession, which has a high regard for his ability as a doctor. He has played an important role in striking a balance between the Government and the doctors. He himself came up through a number of official positions, including a ten-year assignment as doctor at a military hospital in Boden, Sweden's most northern military outpost, followed by a similar period as hospital superintendent in Falun, a provincial town.

Engel was one of the few doctors in Sweden who favored compulsory health insurance but with limitations. He felt the British had gone too far with their panel system and that Swedes ought to be able to choose their own hospital, if not always their own doctor. After a year's experience with the new compulsory insurance, he believes it is working far better than expected and that it has come to stay, although he is critical of some of the provisions and is trying to amend them.

Like everyone else, Engel had anticipated that the transition from the voluntary to the compulsory system would be chaotic, and he was surprised to find that it was accomplished fairly smoothly, with the exception of an initial rush to collect benefits. There was little increased pressure on the hospitals. He ascribes this to the cheapness of hospitalization and medical care before the change. There was some increase of patients in the countryside, mostly among those who were not previously insured, but no great change in the cities. The hospitals were always full, and the only difference is that the waiting time in the countryside was somewhat prolonged. This has now leveled off.

Dr. Engel favors some modifications which would do away with flaws which the operation of the system has revealed. Chief among these is the time consumed for paper work such as reports and accounting, which require an added 10 per cent of the doctor's time, increasing the pressure on the already overworked medical profession. He also regrets that the compulsory health insurance has caused employers to lose interest in medical and welfare schemes for their employees, with resultant injury to the health of industrial workers.

Åke Natt och Dag, Director General of the Government insurance agency which pays out the medical benefits, was no less astonished by the relatively smooth transition. He believes that the confusion which prevailed in England at the outset was avoided because the Swedish system is not completely free. For instance, there is a daily charge of sixty cents for hospitalization which is refunded, but a patient has to make the outlay; there is a fee for most medicines outside of hospitals; and medical care is only three-quarters free. This principle he believes, has acted as a brake.

It is yet too early, in the opinion of Natt och Dag, to assess the cost of the new experiment, but he believes, from the preliminary figures, that it may be less than was reckoned. The total cost of the health insurance was estimated at $160,000,-000 for the first year, and actually cost $65,000,000 for the first six months—$15,000,000 short of the estimate. This does not include all the claims which may be made for this period, so that the figure is not conclusive, but Natt och Dag believes that it reveals the trend. The State contributes 29 per cent of the cost; employers, 27 per cent; and the insurance premiums collected along with the taxes account for the remaining 44 per cent.

Some of the defects which have become apparent in the

system are serious and are causing dissatisfaction. For instance, under the former voluntary system, a worker could be absent during illness and expect his full salary for at least three months; if he was insured, a small additional amount would cover his medical care. But under the present system, his pay ceases within three days and he collects his insurance instead, which represents only about half of his income. In many cases some adjustment is made by employers, but this is a matter between employer and employee and is not compulsory. Thus many workers are less well off than they were before.

Another complaint centers around the limitation of two years' compensation for the same illness. As an example, Mrs. Agda Olsson, a former houseworker now in her fifties, has been suffering from a chronic heart ailment for the past ten years. She faithfully paid her voluntary insurance under the old system for over twenty years. Now she is deprived of any benefits because she has suffered from the same ailment far beyond the two-year limitation. Her only recourse is to apply for an invalid's pension, but she is only entitled to it if she can prove that her working capacity is reduced by two-thirds. She is too young for an old-age pension.

For the permanently disabled, the State grants a small pension and some benefits to meet special needs. The pathetic case of Gösta Eriksson, a young worker prematurely incapacitated, illustrates how a permanent invalid without any resources of his own fares under the welfare program.

Eriksson, who is thirty-one years of age, has a rare confidence in himself and a determination to carry on in the face of adversity. His courage is amazing. Doctors who have examined and treated him have pronounced him incurable and repeatedly sentenced him to death, but he is unwilling to accept their verdict or to believe that he cannot earn a living for himself and his family.

Illness struck Eriksson suddenly. He was working in a store when he contracted spondylosis, a disease of the vertebrae for which the doctors can provide no cure. When he suffered the first attack, he called on a private doctor who advised him to see a specialist. The latter sent him to Southern Hospital, but it was three months before he could gain admission. He has stayed in hospital for four periods of two months each within the past couple of years, but the hospital will not care for him any longer because he is considered incurable. He has been directed instead to a home for the aged, which means marking time until death. He has refused to go there because he believes he will survive.

Eriksson is now back at home with his wife and two young children, boys aged seven and two. Although the doctors have told him that he can never walk again or expect to work, he has set aside his crutches and hobbles around the house. The worst, he says, is that no one will give an invalid a real job, and he wants to work. The Social Welfare Bureau will employ him pasting flags or licking stamps, but this does not satisfy him. So he has started a small business of his own, selling photographic material. This brings in a small income, and he is setting the money aside, knowing that someday he may not be able to continue work.

Because he is considered incapacitated, Eriksson receives a number of benefits, which include an invalid pension of about $35 a month, a special allowance for the "high cost of living," a relief benefit from the municipality, and a small allowance for the children, all of which total $65 a month. This, he says, is "too little to live on but too much to starve on." There is no margin to keep the furniture in repair or to bring any niceties into the home.

Eriksson would like to return to hospital for another short period because he feels the therapy is beneficial, but no hospital will take him. They are overcrowded and it is considered that the chronically ill should not occupy space which can be used to better advantage by those who can recover. Eriksson is naturally bitter about this. He feels the authorities will not help him because they believe he will "never be a taxpayer again." But he remarks, with an indomitable spirit, that the happiest day of his life will come when he can walk erect into the office of the doctors who pronounced his doom and when he can refund to the welfare organizations the benefits he has received.

The Pensions Board believes that day will never come. It has examined his records and is convinced that his case is a hopeless one. Konrad Persson, Director General of the Pensions Board, who asked me to bring to his attention any flaws I might find in the administration of the welfare program, explains that the board is extremely careful to make sure that pensions are granted only to incurables, since the cost of a pension, however small, is considerable over a period of years. He figures that Eriksson, though incurable, may live for many years and may represent a heavy expenditure for the State. He stresses therefore that this is no haphazard judgment and that the State would be glad to restore Eriksson as a useful citizen if medical science considered there was a chance.

Another flaw in the new health insurance was disclosed by an unexpected police strike over the popular midsummer weekend holiday last year. The police, as the arm of the law, are not allowed to strike. But policemen took advantage of the provision in the new health insurance law which continues an employee's pay during the first three days of illness without the need of a medical certificate, and two-thirds of the force reported sick. There was nothing the Government could do about it other than to warn doctors against issuing certificates to "sick" policemen beyond the three-day limit without good reason. That ended the strike. As a matter of principle, an employee need not furnish a medical certificate for a period of a week unless his employer or the Government insurance agency demands it.

Compulsory health insurance has been accepted with the greatest reluctance by the doctors. They opposed it consistently for years, but were overruled by the Government and Parliament. Dr. Dag Knutsson, chairman of the Swedish Medical Association, who led the losing battle, blames the political parties for competing in welfare. He is against compulsion and believes that the medical program should be based on the principle of "helping people to help themselves" and not upon reliance on the state. In a paternalistic state, he says, the spiritual standard is lowered, the individual loses his sense of judgment, and the people are never content but will always demand new benefits. He calls the new compulsory health insurance a "deception" because it gives the people the impression they are obtaining free medical treatment, whereas their payment is actually concealed in indirect taxes. He claims that half of the patients now in hospitals need not be there.

There are now 5,600 doctors in Sweden, approximately eight to every 10,000 people, as compared to fourteen to the same number of inhabitants in the United States. Dr. Knutsson estimates that the new program requires an increase of 30 per cent in doctors, and they will not be available for another ten years. The study period for doctors has already been decreased from eight to six years in an attempt to make up for the shortage, but must result in a lowering of the medical standard.

Dr. Gerda Höjer, President of the Nurses' Association, cannot yet estimate how many more nurses are required. There are now 14,000 nurses in Sweden, but recruiting has been difficult because of the long training period and the poor pay. There was a threat of a nurses' strike back in 1951, and

Parliament was called into emergency session. It threatened to draft the nurses, but a compromise led to a slight pay raise. Nurses, however, are still underpaid in relation to other occupations. A head nurse with three years' basic training and nine years' hospital experience receives $200 a month, about the same as a streetcar conductor. Dr. Höjer believes that the immediate solution to the nursing shortage is to offer part-time jobs to former nurses who are married and have retired.

The medical program extends also to dentistry, with particular emphasis on children. It is felt that if children's teeth are regularly cared for, it will eliminate a great deal of the need for dentistry later on. It is therefore largely a preventive program. Every child up to the age of sixteen is entitled to a dental examination once a year and to necessary care free of charge. This expense is borne jointly by the State and the local county council. Public dentists are required to give a priority to children and to set aside 55 per cent of their time for this purpose.

Adults are treated at public clinics for half the fees charged by private dentists, but there is usually a long waiting period, as the adult requirements are greater than those of the children to which the dentists must devote the greater part of their time. It is figured that this situation will remedy itself in time as the older generation passes out of the picture and the new generation which has benefited from regular dental care will need less attention.

The Swedish people have accepted the change from voluntary to compulsory health insurance without enthusiasm, without protesting, and with a big question mark. There have been very divided opinions, and the general attitude is to wait and see how the system will work out in the long run. The advantages are obvious. The new system has enrolled an extra forty per cent of the population which was not insured either because it could not afford even the very low cost or because it was indifferent. Most of these people were in the lower income group and now have the benefit of medical care they never had before.

On the other hand, the price is higher taxes, both direct and indirect, and the average Swede believes the taxes were high enough before. Many would prefer tax reduction or a halt to taxation to new benefits.

The flaws in the administration of the system will undoubtedly be adjusted in time, but there are more fundamental defects. There is the long waiting period to gain admission to hospitals, the long line-up at public clinics, the pressure on the medical and nursing staffs which cannot but lower the medical standard, the impersonal treatment, and the increased paperwork which spells more bureaucracy.

What many Swedes are asking themselves is: Why was the change necessary? The answer to that question is that the Social Democratic Party had a promise to fulfill.

CHAPTER VIII

Social Welfare—How It Works

THE Swedish welfare program has certain definite characteristics: it is not reserved exclusively for the needy but some benefits are available to all as a right of citizenship; it is not offered as charity, so that there is no stigma attached to it; and it covers a span from the prenatal period when an expectant mother becomes entitled to certain benefits, to the grave, when the State helps with funeral expenses if necessary.

Welfare has now progressed so far in Sweden that Ernst Bexelius, Director General of the Social Welfare Board, is able to make the statement that "there are no slums in Sweden" and "no one is starving or destitute." Few officials anywhere can honestly make such a statement. Bexelius admits that there are many poor homes, but he maintains that they are not slums "in the international sense of the word."

If Sweden has the reputation of being in the forefront in welfare, it is largely due to the efforts of Gustav Möller, who retired in 1951 after serving for two decades as Minister of

Social Welfare, and who personally promoted much of the legislation for social benefits and sponsored all of it. In his task he was assisted by his energetic and dynamic wife, who prefers to be known by her maiden name as Else Kleen. She has been referred to as the "Social Ministress."

Möller's interest in welfare sprang from his own background—that of a poor boy, orphaned at an early age. He was only three years old when his father died and fourteen when his mother died. Möller, like Per Albin Hansson, was born in the outskirts of Malmö in southern Sweden, in a district which, according to his own description, was inhabited by "laborers and ragged proletarians" and where children were accustomed to misery and frequent scenes of drunkenness. When Gustav Möller's father died penniless, his mother had to work as a charwoman, going from house to house cleaning and scrubbing floors for as little as twenty cents a day. Despite her valiant fight for existence, poverty was always close at hand, and when she died at the age of twenty-seven, young Gustav and a brother three years his senior were left to face the world alone. He determined then to fight for better living conditions. "Society offered my mother no help against overwork, illness, and poor housing conditions," he says. "She was overpowered by circumstances and died prematurely. I felt then that something had to be done about it."

Left to his own devices, young Möller took a job as an office boy in a cement factory and eventually became private secretary to the head of the firm. Then, like Branting and Per Albin Hansson, he turned to journalism and politics and became secretary of the Social Democratic Party, a post he held for a quarter of a century. He first entered Branting's cabinet as Social Welfare Minister in 1924, and served almost uninterruptedly in that capacity through successive cabinets until his retirement. Although he had only eight years of elementary schooling, Möller has acquired two honorary degrees in law and medicine respectively from Sweden's leading universities of Uppsala and Lund.

When he reached the retirement age of sixty-seven, he received with particular pride the certificate for his old-age pension, handed to him in a leather folder by the Ministry of Social Welfare—the pension he had worked so hard to obtain for others. It was his legislative bill that made it possible.

Möller is a heavy-set man with bushy eyebrows, a ruddy complexion, gray hair parted close to the center, twinkling blue eyes, and a slow but sure manner which inspires confidence. He speaks English with some hesitation, but he gradually warms up to his subject and becomes enthusiastic and even emphatic. He is an astute politician and came near to becoming Prime Minister on the death of his colleague Per Albin Hansson in 1946. Some say Möller missed that chance because of his overactive wife. Others relate that the party was looking for younger timber when it chose the then obscure Tage Erlander for the leadership.

Although retired from the cabinet, Möller remains one of the key figures in the Social Democratic Party. As the leading authority on social matters, he still exerts a considerable influence on the future course of events in Sweden. With adequate labor, raw materials and capital, he explains, Sweden has the resources with which to banish poverty and want.

Looking back over his two decades at the helm of Sweden's social development, Möller is satisfied that a sound basis has been laid, but he feels that there is yet a great deal to be done. He has been guided by three basic principles which he outlines as follows:

1. He wants legislation to guarantee to every Swedish citizen a simple and decent standard of living. He feels that it is the duty of society to provide for the needs of the aged, invalids, widows, and those who have lost their income through no fault of their own.

2. He insists on housing and child benefits for needy families so that they should not be forced to lower their standard of living because they have children to raise. His idea is to distribute the expense over the entire population as a collective responsibility. This is a matter of maintaining the birth rate as well as keeping up the standard of living for families.

3. Social welfare is to be considered the inherent right of every citizen irrespective of his financial status. This is now the case with the aged, who receive a pension whether they need it or not; with child benefits; hospitalization; and medical care. Möller admits that it is a difficult problem when it comes to pensions for the disabled or invalids, or for those persons living on relief. He wants it to be possible for these people to supplement their pensions by earning money for themselves so they may retain some initiative, but he admits they cannot continue to be a public charge beyond a certain point. That point has never been fixed, and it is one of the big problems yet to be solved.

Else Kleen—Mrs. Möller—is one of the most discussed public figures in Sweden. She is extremely outspoken and entirely unpredictable. Some call her an "extraordinary woman," others call her "incredible." Her sharp wit and even her clothes have created many a sensation in Stockholm society and in court circles. She has strong personal likes and dislikes, and she revels in what she calls being "frank at all times." But whatever opinion one may have of Else Kleen—and opinions are as numerous as her friends and critics—there can be no doubt that she has unbounded energy, determination, and enthusiasm. Her career has marked her as a crusader and reformer. She fought for better treatment for prisoners and chose to go to jail to see conditions from the inside, and she has sponsored a number of projects, foremost among which is an experimental plan for caring for the insane outside of institutions.

For her own life, Else Kleen has chosen the middle way. She is of noble birth but is a Social Democrat like her husband. The story is told that at a Social Democratic gathering she shocked party members by remarking that she was tired of scrubbing floors in "the people's home" (Sweden). In her youth she was reputed to have been a beauty and greatly sought after. Möller is her fourth husband, but she has been married to him for over twenty-five years. Her former husbands were a lawyer, an architect, and a military officer.

Now over seventy, Else Kleen looks fifteen years younger than she is. The secret of her youth is her animation and vitality. Her interests are wide and varied. They range from world affairs to internal politics and her pet social schemes. She speaks fluent English, but frequently lapses into French, interspersing her language with colorful adjectives and even swear words; she has an obvious sense of the dramatic. Else Kleen is listed in *Who's Who* as an author and journalist, and she has written a number of books on such varied subjects as women's clothes, how to be one's maid, care of prisoners, etc., and has contributed fashion articles to the newspaper *Stockholms Tidningen* for the past forty years under the pen name of Gwen.

When I telephoned to Else Kleen for an interview, she replied characteristically, "For heaven's sake, get it over quickly." But when I arrived at the Möller home, she received me most cordially and was in no hurry. In fact, I spent several hours with her. At one point, she called up her husband in his office at the Parliament and asked him to come home and join us. When the telephone operator asked whether she wanted to speak to "Minister Möller," she replied, "No, plain Mr. Möller—he is no longer Minister." Möller reported home within fifteen minutes.

Else Kleen wanted me to understand what her husband had meant when he advocated a "simple and decent" standard of living for all people. She said he meant it to be a comfortable living with running water in all homes. The Swedish people, she said, were not to be judged by monetary standard. "We do not care in the least if people have money or not," she declared with emphasis. "Our social respect has nothing to do with money. Very highly placed persons, whose families have wielded great influence in Swedish history, do not have a penny to their name. But they can live a simple and decent life, if not a clean and comfortable one."

Mrs. Möller takes credit for several prison reforms. She is responsible for legislation whereby prisoners are granted "leave" outside of prison and she has been a strong advocate of a rehabilitation period for prisoners to fit them for normal life after their release. Her own experience of prison life was partly accidental, but she took advantage of the opportunity. She had sponsored a book, published anonymously by a prisoner serving a life sentence for murder, protesting against conditions in Långholmen Prison in Stockholm. The prison authorities sued for libel and she was given a two-month suspended sentence, but she insisted on serving her term in Långholmen Prison, to the great embarrassment of the cabinet and prison authorities. She now relates with glee what consternation the presence of the wife of the Minister of Social Welfare caused prison officials. "They were pale with fright," she says. During her imprisonment even the law under which she was committed was amended, but she served out her sentence. She says it taught her little because she was well acquainted with conditions in advance, but it confirmed her impressions.

The welfare program in Sweden aims to maintain a certain minimum standard of living, or what Mr. Möller calls "a simple and decent" living. This is difficult to define, but it seems to represent a standard approximating that of a poorer laborer or worker. It is intended to insure a healthy, simple life, free from want to the end.

In order to determine how the welfare program works, I observed two contrasting families over a period of five years. I visited them in their homes, talked over their problems with them at intervals, and watched how they dealt with them and how they fared. One family—the Carlssons—has been entirely dependent on public support and would otherwise have been destitute. On the other hand, the Ginsberg family is representative of a poorer worker's family, receiving some benefits but also paying some taxes to the State.

I came upon these families when I received a request from the Columbia Broadcasting System to interview two poor families with contrasting ways of life for a radio program entitled "Freedom from Want." This program was one of a series from a number of European countries, and correspondents in most of the other countries came through with dire tales of misery. But not so in Sweden. I actually had difficulty in locating two poor families and was only able to do so through the intermediary of relief societies.

Mrs. Carlsson, whose husband had left her without any means of subsistence, was the mother of five children. She was unemployed, partly because most of her time was taken up with the children and her household, and partly because she had no incentive to work. She was therefore entirely dependent upon the State and municipality for the support of her family.

The Carlssons lived in a modern apartment house in Enskede, a suburb of Stockholm where there is a settlement for poor people supported by the municipality. The Carlsson apartment on the ground floor consisted of three bedrooms, dinette, kitchen and bathroom, with all windows facing outside. There was a bright and cheerful living room on the front side of the house, facing a broad avenue with a playground beyond it. This room also served as bedroom for Mrs. Carlsson and one child. Two children slept in each of the other two bedrooms. The furniture was sparse but well polished, and everything was clean, neat, and orderly. There were pink curtains in all the rooms, flowerpots on the window sills in the living room, and there was a sprig of ivy growing along the wall. The apartment was steam-heated.

A hundred yards in the rear of the house was the public school which all five Carlsson children attended. There was a ski jump, part of the school's athletic activities, within sight of the house, and there was the co-operative store adjoining the school where Mrs. Carlsson and the entire neighborhood shopped. Mrs. Carlsson could not afford the small fee necessary to join the local co-operative as a member, but that is not required to buy in a co-operative store and she benefited from the low prices.

Mrs. Carlsson was then in her middle forties. She was tall, scrawny, pinched, and obviously worried, but phlegmatic. She seemed to accept her fate and went about caring for the household and the children as a matter of routine. Life held out little to her and she seemed to expect little of it. The children included three boys—Raymond, then nine years old; John, ten; Roland, twelve—and two girls—Marianne, thirteen; and Inga, fifteen. They seemed in good health, although the two younger boys were pale and suffered from a hacking cough. They were plainly clothed. The girls wore woolen sweaters and the boys, thick suits. All had thick stockings and heavy shoes, needed in the cold Scandinavian winter climate. The clothing was supplied free by the school.

Mrs. Carlsson's rent should have been $20 a month, but she paid none because she was unemployed, without income, and the mother of five children—all compelling circumstances. The family enjoyed many free benefits which included schooling for the children through six compulsory grades, a daily lunch at school, summer camp and travel to and from camp at Government expense, a vacation for Mrs. Carlsson in summer, and medical care for the family. For the support of the family, Mrs. Carlsson received $62 a month from the State and municipality. This was sufficient to provide the Carlssons with adequate food and a maintenance, just short of want.

The main trouble was that Mrs. Carlsson was unable to improve her position and that of her family. She could not accept any payment in excess of ten dollars a month without having it deducted from her social benefits. In order to retain more than ten dollars in wages, she would have had to earn more than the $62 she received from the Government and the municipality; that was beyond her earning capacity and would have disqualified her for social welfare. Her earnings as a scrubwoman or houseworker would not have exceeded $30 to $40 a month. Mrs. Carlsson's only way to better herself would have been to remarry, and her chances of doing so with five children to raise, at her age, and in her financial predicament were slight.

Directly above the Carlssons in the same house lived the Ginsberg family, which I selected as a contrasting example because Adolf Ginsberg was a wage earner. He was a typical average middle-aged worker, with a wife and three children. Their apartment was identical with the Carlsson's, their standard of living approximately the same, and the children went to the same school and received the same education; but the Ginsbergs were paying most of their way and the Carlssons were not.

Five years ago Ginsberg was a poor man by Swedish labor standards. Although he had spent some ten years in Canada in the printing business, he was only an assistant printer on the typographical staff of *Dagens Nyheter*, Stockholm's morning liberal newspaper. He earned $80 a month, but he was not entitled to the same benefits as Mrs. Carlsson because he was a wage earner. He received a 40 per cent reduction in rent because he had a family of four to support, but he still had to pay $12 a month. He also paid $2.00 in income tax a month. This left him $66 for the maintenance of his family— only $4 more than Mrs. Carlsson received in relief money, and his children were not entitled to free clothing from the school since they were not destitute. In other words, Gins- berg, the worker, lived no better than Mrs. Carlsson, who was maintained on public funds. And neither Mrs. Carlsson nor Ginsberg were satisfied with this condition. Mrs. Carls- son complained because there was no way for her to better herself and raise the standard of living of her family, and Ginsberg complained because Mrs. Carlsson, on relief, was able to live just as well "doing nothing."

But in the intervening five years, the situation of both families has changed. The Carlssons have managed to get along somehow; the children have grown up so that the eld- est, the two girls, have jobs and contribute to the family sup- port, but Mrs. Carlsson's health has broken down under the strain. On the other hand, the Ginsbergs' economic position has improved. Ginsberg is paid more and he has invested in several types of insurance to protect his future and that of his family. The Ginsberg family is by no means prosperous, but it is secure. They seem to have overcome the worst years and are looking forward to better times.

Mrs. Carlsson is more worn-looking than she was five years ago. Then she was struggling to keep the family going. Now she has grown apathetic. She has had a nervous breakdown and a relative has to come in to do the cleaning and help with the cooking. The apartment is still neat and clean, and the Carlssons have acquired a radio for the entertainment of the family, and an aquarium. The three boys are still in school, while Inga, the eldest daughter. twenty years old, is working in a coat factory in a Stockholm suburb, and Marianne, eighteen, is an apprentice in a clothing store in the city.

Because the two daughters are now wage earners, Mrs. Carlsson's benefits have been cut, so that her budget remains approximately the same despite the fact that the cost of living has risen considerably in the intervening years. She no longer gets free rent, but has to pay $20 a month. This still represents a reduction, as the rent has risen and the full amount would now be $30. The three boys are still clothed free by the school and still go free to summer camp. But Mrs. Carlsson's benefits have been reduced from $62 a month to $22, a cut equal to the amount contributed by the two working daughters for their board and lodging. This means that the Carlsson family is actually somewhat worse off than it was five years ago because prices have risen at least 25 per cent and the benefits have lagged behind. Aside from a life insurance for $240, Mrs. Carlsson has no other insurance benefits.

Mrs. Carlsson takes an occasional job, scrubbing floors, but the rule still holds that she cannot keep any earnings in excess of ten dollars a month, and this has long ago deprived her of any initiative or desire to work.

On the other hand, the Ginsberg picture is a much brighter one. Ginsberg has received several raises in pay in accordance with the rising index in the cost of living. His typographical union has seen to that. And he works at night and is paid overtime. His wages have risen over the five years from $80 a month to $177, a fairly high bracket for a Swedish worker. The eldest boy, Nils, now sixteen, has a job and contributes a small amount for his board and lodging. But despite this relative prosperity, the Ginsbergs have to watch their expenditure carefully because Ginsberg has an income tax of $40 a month to meet; his union dues amount to $6.00; and he has taken out two types of medical insurance, life insurance for the entire family and accident insurance beyond the compulsory amount. The Ginsbergs are therefore well provided against adversity.

The outlook for the Carlssons and the Ginsbergs can best be gauged from their children. I have talked with Marianne Carlsson and Nils Ginsberg in an attempt to gain from them an insight as to their future plans and ambitions. Marianne clearly reflected the apathy of her mother, who raised the children on relief, while Nils displayed the ambition of a workman's son to better himself.

Marianne at eighteen is blond and blue-eyed, with a little upturned nose. She is slim and neatly dressed in a cheap gray suit with black skull cap and black leather bag to match. She is a plain-looking girl. She puts in a forty-eight hour week in a clothing store in Stockholm, where her job is merely to hand clothes to a sales girl and hang them up again. It is a three-year apprenticeship, during which she is supposed to learn something about materials and fashions to qualify as a salesgirl. She earns $60 a month, pays $16 to her mother for board and lodging, $6.00 for transportation, and $8.00 in taxes. That leaves her $30 for clothing and incidentals. She is satisfied with her job, has no ambition to do anything else, has no interest in any extra schooling beyond the six compulsory grades she has gone through, and has no desire to learn any foreign languages or travel abroad.

She is already engaged but prefers not to marry until she is twenty. Her fiancé, three years older, is a clerk and stevedore for a shipping firm and a bus conductor in his spare time during weekends. He, too, is satisfied with his employment and seems to have no special ambition. When they are married, they plan to live with his parents in the suburbs.

Marianne is well mannered and pleasant, but she is just as apathetic toward life as her mother and seems to have developed no particular aptitude. One cannot escape the feeling that if her husband should leave her someday, as her father abandoned her mother, Marianne would be without any particular skill or earning capacity and might well find herself in the same predicament—on relief. It is evident that Mrs. Carlsson's lack of incentive has left its imprint on Marianne.

Nils Ginsberg is a clean-looking boy of sixteen with a frank expression and a zest for life. He is tall, blue-eyed, with wavy blond hair, a typical Swedish youth. He speaks good English which he has learned from his father, who picked it up in Canada years ago. Father and son speak it together. Nils is bubbling over with ambition. He does not quite know in what he will succeed. He would like to be an actor if he has the talent, and he means to find out whether he has it. For the time being, he is working in the interior decorating department of a chain store. It is a four-year apprenticeship, and he intends to take a night course in a theatrical school to qualify eventually for the Dramatic Theater in Stockholm.

At the moment, Nils is making just enough to pay six dollars a week to his parents for board, lodging, and clothing, and to cover his tax and transportation; this leaves him with $2.50 weekly for pocket money. He admits that this is not much, but he realizes that he has to learn a trade and that there is no quick way to success. He has had eight years of schooling in the same school that Marianne attended, although they were not in the same grade, and he has passed the high school finishing examination. He has been to Norway and would like to travel on the European continent, but has no thought of going to the United States because that is far beyond the Ginsbergs' means.

For a boy of his age, Nils is well balanced. He is serious, ambitious to the extent that he wants to make a name for himself; and he feels that life holds out a bright prospect for him if he applies himself and finds the occupation for which he is best fitted.

The paternalistic welfare state has made it possible for the Carlssons to exist with a minimum of hardship, to keep the wolf from the door, and to raise the family to maturity without any major misfortune befalling any of them. It did not provide them with any luxuries, but that was never intended. At the same time, Mrs. Carlsson was prevented from earning a living, although she had time to work outside of the home while the children were away at school. This is what Mr. Möller had in mind when he urged that persons on relief should be able to supplement their benefits to a certain extent, so that they would not lose all initiative. The problem is how much Mrs. Carlsson should have been permitted to earn without losing any of her benefits. Obviously the ten-dollar limit was entirely insufficient.

Five years ago when the Ginsbergs were poor, they too received some help, such as a reduction in rent and some free advantages, but they never received a subsidy as the Carlssons did, so that Ginsberg was never deterred from earning a living. On the contrary, Ginsberg wanted to work and improve the standard of living of his family, and he succeeded. In other words, it still pays to work in the welfare state, if not deprived of the opportunity as Mrs. Carlsson was. But there are too many cases like that of the Carlssons. Some are victims of circumstances beyond their control. Others have grown apathetic, in the belief that it is the duty of the State to provide for them as a right of citizenship.

CHAPTER IX

Child Welfare

CHILD WELFARE is administered by a special board, known as the Child Welfare Board, with local committees established in every municipality throughout Sweden. It is supervised by the Ministry of Social Welfare. The board has very extensive powers: it acts when called upon for assistance, but it may also intervene on its own authority, even against the will of the parents, if it seems necessary for the protection of a child. The board's paramount concern is the welfare of the child, and this is the primary consideration in any action it may take.

The local committees are appointed by the provincial councils, elected every four years by popular vote. In rural communities these committees consist of at least five members and include a member of the local Board of Public Assistance, a clergyman, a schoolteacher, a doctor, and a lawyer; one of the members must be a woman. This is considered a solid cross section of any local community. In the larger cities, such as Stockholm, a number of trained social workers and experts are also members of the board.

The Child Welfare Board has jurisdiction over all minors until at least eighteen years of age, and in some cases up to twenty-one. Its duties include the care of needy children and of delinquents. In delinquency cases the board functions in close co-operation with the courts; there are no juvenile courts in Sweden. The board provides homes for orphaned and other infants whose mothers are unable to care for them; homes for new mothers where they can be with their babies; homes for children who are a public charge; and foster homes for thousands of children whose parents are unable to care or provide adequately for them. Approximately 35,000 children are brought up in foster homes under the supervision of the board.

There are no private institutions for the care of children. Whatever private organizations or homes were in existence have been taken over in recent years by the State, which is now responsible for every form of aid to children. The largest institution for problem children maintained by the Child Welfare Board is the Nyboda home in the outskirts of Stockholm, which serves as a clearing center for two hundred children; they are taken in temporarily for observation before they are sent to other institutions or placed in foster homes. These children's ages range from one to sixteen years old. They are children of unwed mothers or of parents who are unable to care for them, or children who have been removed from their homes because they were maltreated and who require a change of environment. Parents who can afford it are charged thirty cents a day for the maintenance of a child, but there is no charge if the parents are considered too poor to pay.

The children at Nyboda are placed under close observation when they first enter the institution. Their background is checked, and they are examined physically and mentally to determine what shall eventually be done with them. Those who are of normal intelligence attend the neighborhood school, while there are special classes at Nyboda for backward children.

Although the home is clean, orderly, and efficiently run, with the maximum of freedom for the children, Nyboda is, of course, not without its tragedies. For instance, there is Eva, the willowy little blond girl in a check dress, with upturned nose and sad gray eyes. She is eight years old but is a backward child with an I.Q. of only 60. She is exceptionally sensitive and affectionate and craves attention. Although the other children accept her as one of them, she prefers to play with the younger ones—the four year olds. That is her mental level.

Eva's background is typical of many at Nyboda. Her mother is unmarried and has to work to support herself and the child. When her mother went to work, Eva was left with her grandmother. But now she has reached the compulsory age for schooling and does not fit into the regular schools. There is a public school for backward children, but it is too far from Eva's home and she is unable to make her way alone. In despair, her mother appealed to the authorities, and Eva was taken into Nyboda for observation. She has been examined physically and mentally, and it has now been decided to send her to Slagsta, a boarding school for the mentally deficient. When the popular superintendent Ivar Lidman, who knows each child personally, enters the room, Eva clings affectionately to him, and when he eventually pushes her gently aside, she cries. It is evident that Eva needs the love that no institution can provide and that her mother has no time to give her.

Then there is Lajla, the lively, intelligent little brunette with the heart-shaped face. She is nine years old and far above average intelligence. She is tops in her class in the community school and is full of fun and, particularly, mischief.

She will open the door to the quarantine and let the sick children out, she will pick up the telephone wherever she may be and hang it up again, she will scatter sand in the corridors and be involved in a score of other pranks. And what is worst for the staff, Lajla is a leader among the children and drags them into all kinds of trouble too.

Lajla's home background is also a tragic one. Her father is a hard-working laborer, but her mother is schizophrenic and has been in and out of mental institutions for years. Last Christmas Lajla was allowed to go home for a couple of weeks, but no sooner had she stepped into the house than her mother, who has a persecution complex apparently directed against the little girl, beat her. So instead of spending the holiday with her parents, Lajla had to return to Nyboda and spend it virtually alone, since most of the other children had gone home. Superintendent Lidman is trying to find a good foster home for Lajla. Careful observation has given the doctors no reason to believe that she has inherited any of her mother's symptoms, but she is a nervous child, as might well be expected under the circumstances.

Lidman and other officials of the Child Welfare Board consider that Nyboda is too big an institution and that difficult children should be cared for in much smaller homes which do not have the character of an institution and where they can be given more individual attention. It is planned that homes where children are to be kept over a period of years shall not accommodate more than fifteen children.

An experimental home of this type has just been completed at Orby, close to Nyboda. It had only seven children at the time I visited it. This home resembles a large private house and there is nothing either from the outside or inside to mark it as an institution. It is a two-story dwelling, resembling any of the better country homes, with spacious living quarters on the ground floor and half a dozen bedrooms on the second floor, accommodating from one to three children in each, with luxurious tiled bathrooms adjoining. The rooms are gaily furnished with bright chintz curtains and modern light wood furniture, and there is a punctilious neatness about everything. The home scarcely looks lived in. Certainly these children of poor families were never accustomed to such surroundings. The building was completed at a cost of $110,000 and the maintenance is figured at six dollars a day per child, so that the project represents a very considerable expense to the Swedish taxpayer. This is the kind of experiment which Swedish welfare authorities are prepared to try out and discard if it does not work.

To care for the maximum of fifteen children, there is a staff of five adults, including a woman superintendent who is a trained psychologist, an assistant superintendent, a teacher, a cook, and a maid. The children are backward boys and girls, ranging in age from seven to thirteen. They are considered difficult children who cannot be placed in foster homes or in institutions and who are expected to remain until they are old enough to make their own way in life. It is the hope of the welfare authorities that these children can eventually be fitted to a normal existence and that they may be able to earn their living in some practical occupation even if they are mentally underdeveloped.

An indication of the widespread activities of the Child Welfare Board is that it dealt with over 60,000 children in one way or another during the past year. In close to half of these cases the board did no more than give a warning to the parents or the children. Of this number, 10,000 children were taken into protective custody—placed in institutions, special schools, or under the supervision of a guardian. During 1954, 950 children were removed from their homes by the Child Welfare Board because it considered they were not receiving the right kind of treatment or because they were delinquents;

of this number, at least one-quarter were taken against their parents' will. There were no accurate figures regarding the board's forcible intervention, but some idea may be gained from the number of cases which come before the provincial councils, a requirement when the board takes action which is opposed by the parents. Many, however, never reach the provincial councils, as they are frequently settled before the case gets that far.

The Child Welfare Board is authorized to remove any child from his home and take over the responsibility for his upbringing if it finds that the child is neglected or maltreated by his parents, if there is danger to his health, mental or physical, or if it considers that a child is a delinquent or even likely to become one. The board may intervene if the parents are irresponsible, if the mother is known to be a prostitute, if either of the parents is an alcoholic, or simply because it considers that the living conditions are unhealthy. It may act upon the report of some public authority or even of a private citizen, not infrequently the neighbors.

Before taking drastic action, the board usually warns the parents or attempts to obtain their agreement. But if the board finds that the parents are unwilling to co-operate, it may step in without further ado. This has at times aroused considerable criticism and adverse publicity, and on occasion local boards have been accused of acting arbitrarily and unjustly. Many Swedes are opposed to the idea that some authority can enter their homes and carry off their children, no matter what the circumstances. Many argue that children are better off at home than in an institution or a foster home selected by the Child Welfare Board, which may give rise to difficulties in the future if the foster parents grow fond of the children, as they often do, and are unwilling to surrender them. In such cases of conflict, the courts generally side with the parents, while the Child Welfare Board supports the foster parents. This is a problem which is now claiming the attention of welfare authorities, and two new proposals are under consideration, both favoring the foster parents. One would set a five-year limit, after which the actual parents would lose the right to their children, while the other would make it easier and quicker for foster parents to adopt children than is now possible.

The case of the Bengtsson family, in which four children were forcibly removed from a poor farm laborer's home, has attracted nation-wide attention and has turned out to be a defeat for the Child Welfare Board, which was compelled to return the children to their parents. In order to obtain a comprehensive picture of this case I have interviewed the Bengtssons in their home with their children. I also talked with their lawyer, Baroness Ruth Stjernstedt, a leading feminist; with Erik Kinell, the official in charge of the case in the Child Welfare Board; and with Bengt Jerneck, who has been appointed by the board as a guardian for the Bengtsson children.

Arne Bengtsson is a farmhand in his middle forties. He is married and the father of four children: Barbro, a thirteen-year-old girl who is suffering from a serious heart ailment and may not live, and three boys: Nils Arne, seven; Rolf, four; and Bo, eighteen months old. Bengtsson looks after the pigs on a farm which is located at Farsta, about ten miles outside of Stockholm. It is Government-owned property, administered by two tenant farmers.

The Bengtsson home is a wooden bungalow painted dark red with a white framework. It is located about a quarter of a mile from the main road on flat sandy soil. The outlook is bleak, particularly in winter, when the wind blows mercilessly across the landscape. It is a two-room house consisting of living room and bedroom, but the Bengtssons also use the kitchen as an extra bedroom. According to old Swedish custom, particularly in the country, the Bengtssons reserve the living room for special occasions and do not use it for sleeping, although there is a sofa which might well serve as a bed. This is the largest room, with a double window, and it is sparsely furnished. There is the usual set of furniture: a dining-room table, sideboard, and a couple of stuffed chairs. On the wall there are family portraits, including a colored picture of Mr. and Mrs. Bengtsson on their wedding day fourteen years ago. There is a gilt clock on the wall and a radio-gramophone by the window, described by Mrs. Bengtsson as their two luxuries. The Bengtssons occupy the bedroom with the baby, while the three other children sleep in the kitchen alongside the gas stove and the two boys share one bed. In all my wanderings about Sweden, this is the poorest home I have been in. But it is decent and livable, and it has such modern conveniences as electric light, oil heating, and hot and cold running water.

The reason for the relative poverty of the Bengtsson home is not apparent, for the farmer earns $120 a month, and this is supplemented by an annual allowance from the State of $58 for each child. This gives the Bengtssons a yearly income of $1,672, which is far more than that of many poor families I have visited in Sweden who live in much better circumstances. And Bengtsson's rent is only seven dollars a month.

Bengtsson is a tall, blond, muscular Swede. He is morose and said to be hot-tempered. He is a man of few words, but he knows the details of his household. His wife is tall, energetic, talkative, and obviously brighter than he is. Both are bitter, ill adjusted on the farm, where they keep to themselves, and are resentful of their experience at the hands of the Child Welfare Board. Bengtsson complains about everything and seems to suffer from a persecution complex. He is not only critical of his own living conditions, but he claims that his pigs have been poisoned, and that the milk is polluted.

The children are all below average in mentality. The daughter, Barbro, is pitifully emaciated, not from undernourishment but because of her heart ailment. She was born a blue baby, as was one other child, a boy who died at the age of two. Barbro has undergone a major operation and has been examined by Sweden's two leading heart specialists, Professor Crafoord and Professor Nylin, who both agree that there is nothing more that can be done for her and that the chances of her survival are slight. The other three children are pale. The baby seems to be the healthiest, but it is too early to say whether he is normal or backward like the other children.

The Bengtssons' trouble with the authorities dates back a couple of years to the time when a public nurse, who had gone with Barbro on a periodic visit to a Stockholm hospital, left the child at the main road on a dark and rainy night instead of accompanying her the entire way home. Barbro was frightened and ran the remainder of the way home, arriving drenched. As a result of this experience, she was ill for several days and the parents complained to the hospital.

Last spring, Mrs. Bengtsson was hospitalized for several weeks and later underwent an operation for goiter. On both those occasions the Child Welfare Board, acting at the request of the local clergyman's wife, sent a day worker to the Bengtsson home to assist with the household and the children. A teacher was also sent to coach Barbro, whom the authorities considered too ill to attend regular school. Bengtsson objected to the strange women in his home who, he felt, interfered with his regular routine. After some weeks, both the houseworker and the teacher refused to continue calling at the Bengtsson home, claiming that the father's temper was unbearable. Bengtsson admits that he has a temper but denies that he ever acted violently.

On several occasions during this period, the Child Welfare authorities attempted to persuade both Mr. and Mrs. Bengtsson that they should turn over their children to the care of the board for "protective upbringing" in an institution or foster home. The Bengtssons consistently refused to give up their children or to sign any documents.

One morning last June, just after the return of Mrs. Bengtsson from hospital following her operation, two cars drove up to the Bengtsson home with a party of ten officials. They included three women—a doctor, a representative of the Child Welfare Board, and a policewoman—and seven men—two inspectors, three plain-clothes men, and the two chauffeurs. They came to remove the Bengtsson children to the Nyboda home. They offered no explanation, but they allowed the parents to accompany the children to the institution. In a formal charge, the Bengtssons were later notified that the Child Welfare Board had taken this action because it considered that the children were not being brought up as they should be.

Ignorant of the actual reason for the board's action, the Bengtssons collected affidavits from farmworkers and acquaintances to show that they had not maltreated their children, that there was no quarrel between husband and wife, frequently a reason for interference by the authorities, and that they were both sober and home-loving. The Bengtssons neither drink nor smoke.

The removal of the Bengtsson children from their home was prominently featured by an evening tabloid, which carried on a campaign for the return of the children to their parents. The case aroused widespread public indignation and the Child Welfare Board received scores of protests by mail and telephone. Baroness Stjernstedt, a leading woman lawyer and philanthropist, carried the case to Governor Hagander of Stockholm, who reversed the decision of the Child Welfare Board and ordered the children released—with the understanding, however, that they be placed under the supervision of a public guardian. The case had to be referred to the Governor since the law provides that the provincial council must approve the Child Welfare Board's action in case the parents oppose it, and the Governor is the corresponding authority in the Stockholm area.

The Bengtssons put in a claim with the Child Welfare Board for compensation for legal and other expenses amounting to $300, and have since received $440 in payment. They claim this is "hush money" because the board feels it acted wrongly and is anxious to avoid further unfavorable publicity. It has enabled the Bengtssons to pay off some of their debts, including overdue installments on their furniture.

The Bengtssons now plan to move to Norrköping, a city on the main line south of Stockholm, to get away from the criticism and unpleasantness which the case has stirred among neighbors and fellow workers. They want to make a fresh start. They will also be moving out of the jurisdiction of the Stockholm Child Welfare Board.

Inspector Kinell, who was along when the Bengtsson children were taken to Nyboda, says the board acted because of "the violent temper" of the father, which it considered was a danger to the health of the children, particularly the sick daughter. It acted, too, because the helpers whom it sent to the Bengtsson home during the mother's illness and absence in hospital were unwilling to remain on the job. Kinell maintains that it was not the board's intention to deprive the Bengtssons permanently of their children, since the mother was considered a capable person when she was around.

There seems to be no evidence that the children were ever

maltreated by their parents. During my three-hour visit in the Bengtsson home the children seemed on friendly terms with their parents, and Bo, the baby, sat all the time on his father's lap. The children used bad language, certainly learned in the home, much to the embarrassment of the mother, who repeatedly apologized. They were well clothed, but obviously cleaned and dressed for the occasion. It is impossible to say whether they were well fed, but they were allowed to share the cakes and cookies which Mrs. Bengtsson had prepared and served with coffee.

Bengt Jerneck, a private citizen who has been appointed by the Child Welfare Board as guardian for the Bengtsson family and who does it as a public service, believes there was no good reason for the board to have taken the children from their home. He admits that the father is ignorant, stubborn, and is unable to get along with anyone, but says that he never maltreated the children although he swore at them and at everyone else. He feels that the board acted largely on hearsay and unconfirmed reports from the woman helper and the teacher, who were annoyed at the father's overbearing manner.

Ivar Lidman, the superintendent at Nyboda who had charge of the Bengtsson children there and who had frequent talks with their parents, believes that Bengtsson has changed his "rough manner," knowing that the board can step in and take his children away if he does not behave. Lidman strongly defends the right of the board to intervene in such cases, an attitude which is endorsed by most welfare officials. Miss Christina Ellwyn, a prominent social worker and a former delegate on the Human Rights Commission at the United Nations, believes the board acts "in too few cases rather than in too many."

It seems to be the concensus of opinion that in this case the Child Welfare Board acted without a thorough knowledge of the circumstances. Board officials apparently realized their mistake and did not appeal against the decision of the Governor, although they were entitled to do so. It is evident that the standard of living maintained by the Bengtssons was below that of an average farmhand, although Bengtsson was paid a standard wage, considered sufficient to raise a family. The fault seems to have been with the Bengtssons' inability to manage their own affairs and their finances and with the farmer's arrogant attitude. The outlook for the Bengtsson children—and that is the main consideration in the eyes of Swedish welfare authorities—is an unhappy and a tragic one. Barbro may not survive, but it is certainly questionable whether she would be any better off in an institution than at home, since medical science can apparently do nothing more for her. As for the other children, they will require the special type of schooling provided for backward children, but that does not mean that they need to be placed in an institution, and it is unlikely that any foster home could be found for them. The best solution would seem to be for the Norr-köping Child Welfare Committee to appoint a new guardian there who would have the time and patience to advise the Bengtsson family and who could call on the committee for assistance if need be, for it is unlikely that the Bengtssons will be able to manage any better on their own in the future than in the past. But Mr. Jerneck, their present guardian, will testify that this is a most thankless task.

Consideration for the welfare of the child in Sweden starts in the prenatal period. Abortions have been legal in certain cases since 1938 and the law was amended in 1946 to make it easier for women to obtain legal abortions, with a view to reducing the number of illegal operations. A special committee has been established in the Royal Medical Board to which women seeking abortions may apply. Each case is considered from both medical and social angles, with an increasing disposition to look upon the social conditions as part of the medical picture. In other words, the committee considers medical and hereditary factors and also the living conditions of the woman and whether she is capable of raising a child. The law regarding abortions is probably one of the most liberal in the world. According to the Ministry of Social Welfare, the population policy is based on the principle "of having only desired children," but this has not been accepted by the medical profession, and it is the doctors who decide.

Dr. Verner Westberg, chairman of the committee on abortions, believes that the broadening of the law and the committee's work have had a beneficial effect in reducing the number of illegal abortions. No exact figures are, of course, available regarding illegal abortions, but they are estimated at between 10,000 and 20,000 a year. Legal abortions, on the other hand, are relatively few. Last year 6,079 women applied for legal abortions, of which 4,792 were sanctioned, or 78 per cent. The committee is satisfied that it was able to persuade over a thousand women to give birth to their children and that less than 2 per cent of those whose applications were rejected are known to have resorted to illegal operations. If the maximum figure of 20,000 illegal abortions is correct, the ratio of the total number of women who obtained abortions in Sweden last year to the number of births (105,-396) was one to four.

According to Swedish law, abortions may be legally performed under four headings: medical, "social-medical," humanitarian, and hereditary. Under the medical and hereditary classifications, an abortion may be performed if a woman is suffering from a serious illness or a physical defect which would endanger her life at the time of childbirth, or if there is reason to believe that insanity would be hereditary or that the child would suffer a serious physical debility. For example. if a woman contracts German measles during pregnancy, or is even exposed to it, an abortion can be performed because the child is liable to be born with some physical defect. Abortions for social reasons are still prohibited by law, but the conditions under which the expectant mother is living and her economic circumstances may be considered a mental or physical obstacle for the mother and child.

The humanitarian provision is the broadest and provides that an abortion may be legally performed in cases of rape, incest, and if the woman is pressured by her teacher, adoptive father, guardian, or by a doctor or an official of an institution where she is receiving care; if she is under eighteen and becomes pregnant by "a man who misuses his position as her superior"; and if she is under fifteen, no matter what the circumstances.

Dr. Westberg is strongly opposed to the idea that abortions, legal or illegal, should be considered murder. He contends that this is a dangerous way of thinking which may have a harmful psychological effect on the woman for a prolonged time, or even permanently.

Punishment for those who perform illegal abortions in Sweden is relatively light and ranges from six months' to two years' imprisonment at hard labor; but an abortionist who makes a regular business of illegal operations may be sentenced to six years. A woman who was found to have performed three illegal operations, resulting in the death of one client, was recently sentenced by a Stockholm court to only two years' imprisonment at hard labor, although this was not her first offense.

Under Swedish law, illegitimate children have almost the same rights as other children. Between 11,000 and 12,000 children were born out of wedlock last year, over 10 per cent of the total number of births. There has been a decline in the rate of illegitimacy over the past twenty years, when it was as high as 15 per cent, but this was partly due to the fact that country folk did not take the trouble to legalize their relationship. Probably half the children born out of wedlock are later legitimatized when the parents marry.

The law stipulates that, whenever possible, the paternity of an illegitimate child should be ascertained and the father compelled to contribute to his support, at least until he attains the age of sixteen and, if he can afford it, later. The amount of this support is determined by the Child Welfare Board, based on the father's income, and is generally fixed at about 10 per cent of his earnings. In cases where the father is wealthy, the amount may include a full education for the child through college or a professional school. In the event of the father's death, the obligation devolves upon his heirs. Illegitimate children inherit from the mother, but pending legislation would give them the same rights of inheritance from the father as other children.

The paternity of the child is established in over 90 per cent of all cases. If there is any doubt, a blood test is taken of the supposed father and the child, and if the result is not negative, the man is held responsible. While these blood tests were not conclusive in the past, they are now considered to be fairly accurate. A recent decision of the Swedish Supreme Court attracted considerable attention. It ruled that a man was the father of one twin but not of the other. The Supreme Court based its decision on laboratory tests and a certificate from the Medical Board that this was entirely possible. The man who had been supporting two little girls, now five years old, was freed by this decision from supporting one of them.

Another man, who had been supporting a child for eleven years on the basis of an old blood test, recently asked for a new test, which revealed that he was not the father of the child and relieved him of the responsibility of further support. There was no question, however, of any refund for the contribution he had already made.

A guardian is appointed by the Child Welfare Board for every child born out of wedlock. First, the guardian must assist the mother in her efforts to establish the paternity of the child. The mother is not compelled to admit the identity of the father, but the fact that he is to assume the responsibility for the child's support is generally persuasive. Once the father has been found, it is the duty of the guardian to negotiate a settlement with him for the support of the child, and any such agreement has the same binding effect as a court order. If a father fails to live up to his agreement, the Child Welfare Board may attach his salary. In an extreme case where the father is unemployed or refuses to work, he may be put to work in an institution and the amount withheld from his pay. Such cases, however, are rare, and there were only sixty men working compulsorily in institutions last year, either because they could not or would not contribute to the support of their children. There is no escape within the Scandinavian area, for Sweden has entered into agreements with Norway, Denmark, and Finland to compel fugitive fathers to pay up.

Complications, however, do arise. There is, for instance, the case of Mrs. Halvy Dahl—she calls herself Mrs. because she is a mother, though unmarried. Mrs. Dahl has an eight-year-old son who is the pride and focus of her life. The father, a contractor, admitted the paternity of the boy and made the usual agreement, setting aside 10 per cent of his salary for his son's support. But since then the father has married and has had several more children. He claims he cannot afford to pay for the illegitimate child. Mrs. Dahl has carried her case to the Supreme Court, which has ordered the father to pay. But the law also protects his own family, which has a priority over all other obligations, and welfare authorities have had to admit that the father's income is insufficient for all the demands made upon him. The State has therefore had to intervene and advance a small monthly sum to Mrs. Dahl for her child's support which it hopes someday to recover from the father, if and when he can afford it.

In the meantime Mrs. Dahl is having a difficult time making ends meet. She has a one-room apartment in what is called "a home for self-supporting women with children," which is a fancy name for a home for unwed mothers in order to remove the stigma of illegitimacy. Mrs. Dahl pays only $20 a month rent in this State-subsidized institution. She once worked as a children's nurse, later as a factory worker in a textile plant; but now, due to repeated illness, she is only able to work part-time as a charwoman. During prolonged periods of illness she has received free hospitalization and the boy was cared for at the Nyboda home, but there was no provision for paying the rent at home while mother and child were away, and Mrs. Dahl could not sublet with any chance of getting her apartment back due to the housing shortage. In such instances she has had to turn to the local Board of Public Assistance, but she hesitates to do that, even in extreme need, because she feels "it is asking for charity."

CHAPTER X

Care of the Aged

THE care of the aged in Sweden is largely in the hands of the State and the municipalities. It is regarded as one of the most important aspects of the welfare program. It is a relatively new problem since medical science has enabled people to live longer and there is a new category of aged to be cared for. It is a most controversial problem, for it raises the question of whether the responsibility for care of the aged rightly rests with the State or is the obligation of individual families. There are effective arguments on both sides.

There is evidence to show that in olden times the aged in Sweden were discarded. In heathen days, according to Ivar Lo-Johansson, one of Sweden's leading authors who has specialized on the subject of old age, the aged were done away with either by throwing them over a precipice or by clubbing them to death. The author affirms that this was not considered murder but was a ritual. An old person who was no longer able to look after himself and had become a burden to the family was thrown over a cliff into a lake below, where the body was "purified." Thus the deceased was supposed to attain Valhalla in the same way as a hero killed on the field of battle. In some instances the aged person was beaten to death with a wooden hammer. This was a ceremony in which all members of the family took part so that no blame attached to any one in particular. The nearest relatives held the long wooden handle of the hammer, with the oldest standing closest to the victim. Ivar Lo-Johansson claims that the latest clubbing of this kind occurred as recently as the beginning of the nineteenth century. It seems that only the poor used this method of getting rid of the aged, since the wealthy were able to assume the burden.

The State stepped into the picture about fifty years ago when the first homes for the aged were built. Now there are approximately 1,500 old-age homes in Sweden, caring for over 40,000 people. The State provides a pension for every Swedish citizen reaching sixty-seven years of age, whether he needs it or not. Although it is paid to everyone, irrespective of their financial standing, it is largely taxed away from the rich. This pension is a flat sum of $350 a year for a single person and $560 for a married couple if both have reached the pension age. It is augmented to cover housing, heating, and other necessities and to adjust the total amount to the cost-of-living index, which has been steadily rising. For an elderly couple living in Stockholm, where the cost of living is the highest in the country, these extra benefits bring the total to approximately $1,000 a year. This is just sufficient to support a couple, short of want. The basic pension is also sufficient, even without the supplements, to maintain a couple in an old-age home operated by the State or municipality. In that case, there is no housing allowance and the other supplements are small if there are any. For anyone with an income of $300 a year or more, the benefits are scaled down.

If the new home for the aged at Sabbatsberg hospital in

Stockholm is an example of what Sweden intends to provide for the aged in the future, it is something of a utopia come true in its technical perfection. It is a model which any country might well strive to emulate. The hundred residents of this $300,000 institution are indeed privileged. Although the home is on the grounds of a hospital and is actually a part of it, it is run like a private apartment house. It is built in the most modern achitectural style, with all rooms facing outward, bright glass-enclosed porches, and comfortable public rest rooms on every one of the seven floors. Every inmate has a private room with toilet, washbasin, and kitchenette. The rooms are small but bright, airy, scrupulously clean, and neatly furnished with modern Swedish furniture. There is a radio in every room, potted plants on the windowsills, and here and there a canary in a golden cage. An alarm in every room, the only sign of a hospital, connects with the office of two resident nurses. If the inmates do not want to do their own cooking, or are unable to, there is a public dining room. The whole atmosphere is one of orderliness, efficiency, and the most minute attention to detail. It provides a picture post card view of old age: women with snow-white hair, dressed in their aprons, knitting or sewing or just looking out the window aimlessly; old men with stiff high collars and tight-laced boots, fumbling with some worn papers or doing some handiwork with the pride of a child. Everyone is occupied with his own little task while the days and seasons pass idly by, with only the change of the weather or the span of day and night, so marked in the northern countries.

The inmates are plain people, mostly former workmen. The average age is between seventy and eighty. They have been admitted because they could no longer look after themselves. Most of them are now single—widows or widowers. There are only half a dozen married couples. For instance, there is Mr. and Mrs. Axel Siden. He is eighty-three, a former bricklayer, proud of his trade and particularly proud of the fact that he had a hand in building the House of Parliament. That gives him something of a distinction. It was then that he fell from a ladder and was permanently invalided. The Sidens share a small but cheerful room on the top floor with two windows looking out over the driveway along Lake Mälaren—Stockholm's "Riverside Drive." They spend their day listening to the radio or looking out at the view. There is not much else to do. But they consider themselves fortunate because they have been admitted to the new model home. And they have each other, and that is more than most of the others have. Next door to the Sidens is an old man in his eighties. Thirty years ago he was mixed up in a brawl, killed a man, and was sent to a mental institution. When he was released, he was transferred to the old people's home. Now he spends his time moving about his room, always trying to find a better light to read in. He is not exactly blind, but this is one of his peculiarities. His mustache, flat feet, and his derby hat on top of the closet recall the familiar figure of Charlie Chaplin. Farther down the hall there is Agnes Eklund. She is in her late seventies and she is busy making chair covers. She wants you to admire them and stay and talk with her. She is lonely, and visitors are few and far between.

The old people are told that this is their home and that they are free to go and come as they please. But this is more illusion than reality. As their maintenance absorbs all but five dollars a month of their State pension, they are virtually immobilized, since no one with any private income is accepted at Sabbatsberg.

The chronically ill—and they represent half of the aged inmates at Sabbatsberg—are kept in regular hospital wards. In this section of the hospital there are anywhere from two to six persons in a room, according to the state of their health. An attempt is made to separate the mentally ill from the rest, but this is not always possible because of lack of space. There are also younger patients in the old-age hospital. They are the incurables—such as Gösta Eriksson—who are refused admission to regular hospitals because it would impede the turnover.

Aside from hospitals and the old-age institutions, there are apartments for the aged, maintained by the State and the municipalities, where the old people enjoy considerably more freedom. There are several model colonies of this type in and around Stockholm. In Nockeby, a suburb of the capital, there is a settlement consisting of a score of two-story apartment houses where 220 old people are accommodated. A requirement for admission is that they shall have virtually no income of their own and be dependent, therefore, on the State pension.

Like the new home at Sabbatsberg hospital, this settlement is an example of social welfare at its very best. There is the characteristic neatness and precision about it. Everything seems to be exactly in its right place according to plan. The apartments are small but adequate. They are bright, with large bay windows. Those on the back look out on landscaped gardens. The apartments for married couples consist of two rooms, kitchen, and toilet, and those for single persons, of one room and kitchenette. Almost all have private telephones. The old people have their own furniture, do their own cooking, and lead their own lives without supervision. There is a hostess for the settlement but she is not there in the capacity of a nurse but as an administrator to collect the rent and look after the upkeep. The rent for an apartment for a single person is only four dollars a month and for a married couple, six dollars. The average electric bill, including cooking, is about one dollar a month, and food is estimated at about $20 a month for a couple, so that these old people have a fair margin of their pension left over to buy clothing, go in and out of town, and do some small shopping. This gives them an independence which the old people at Sabbatsberg do not have. They are also permitted to take odd jobs to supplement their income, though most of them are too old. In case of sickness, they are taken to hospital, where they receive free medical treatment; in the event they become chronically ill, they are removed to an old-age institution, where they are cared for. There is a waiting list for admission to Nockeby which is ten times the number of its tenants, and the waiting time is approximately seven years.

There is a public room where occasional entertainment is provided, but there is little community life and emphasis is placed rather on the individualistic character of the establishment. Notwithstanding the seemingly ideal conditions, many of the old people complain that they are surrounded only by the aged and that they feel as if they were shelved. For that reason Nockeby may be the last settlement of its kind. To overcome this objection, it is now planned that the municipalities shall set aside a number of apartments for the use of the aged in new dwellings so that they may feel they are still an integral part of society. The Social Welfare Board would pay the rent and collect the minimum rental from the aged. The deficit would be met by the municipalities, as is now the case at Nockeby and elsewhere.

But there is another side to the old-age picture in Sweden, and it is by no means ideal. Sabbatsberg and Nockeby are models, but there are many old-age homes that date from the turn of the century and have no resemblance to these modern institutions. There is, for instance, Rosenlund in Stockholm, the largest home for the aged in Sweden. Ironically, it is almost across the street from the ultramodern Southern hospital. Rosenlund is no showplace, nor is it willingly shown to visitors even if they learn of its existence. It accommodates 800 patients in its barracklike buildings, erected around a quadrangular courtyard. This is the home of a thousand tragedies and it strikes one with indelible impact.

Rosenlund is divided into three sections: an old age home for the "healthy," a section for the chronically ill, and a hospital ward. The distinction between sections is merely a technicality, for it seems that all the inmates of Rosenlund are suffering from infirmities of some kind and it is only a matter of degree. The home for the healthy is known as "the Golden Wedding Home" because it was built from a fund collected on the occasion of King Oscar II's golden wedding anniversary. Rosenlund dates back to 1887, though additions have been made at intervals and some of the quarters were renovated in the twenties.

There is the same cleanliness about Rosenlund that is to be found all over Sweden, but not the same orderliness, for the institution is so overcrowded that patients are lying everywhere. In the Golden Wedding wing the inmates are for the most part elderly couples. The rooms are large, with high ceilings, but there are no private toilets or kitchenettes. At meal hours, the inmates line up with a tin can and soup is poured into it as they pass the kitchen window to pick up their food. These old people, who are supposed to be in reasonably good health considering their age, are of all sorts. Many walk with canes, or support one another, many are more or less blind, some are talkative though no one listens to them, others are sullen and silent. There is not a smile on any face, for there is not a ray of hope among them. Many are in rags, for they have not enough money left over to buy clothes. This is the poorhouse at its worst, for here are gathered under a single roof all the miseries and sorrows that a lonely, penniless old age brings with it.

The other sections are even worse. In the home for the chronically ill, the old people wander about the hallways,

maimed and distorted, some of them shaking with their af-
flictions. The insane may not be among them, but that is a
fine distinction, for there are many whose minds no longer
function. They may not be dangerous to the rest, but they
are perhaps the greatest tragedy of all. One cannot help won-
dering what medical science achieves in prolonging the lives
of people who have, in fact, ceased to live. Death seems to
lurk everywhere in the hallways of Rosenlund, and one cannot escape the feeling that many would welcome an earlier
end to their sufferings.

Worst of all is the hospital section. There the sick and the
insane lie in wards, six in a room, or in cubicles without
a window and with a blanket hung over the doorway, or
even on cots in the hallways. An old woman in a wheelchair
shouts at the superintendent. He ignores her. "I am not
crazy," she protests, "I have been discharged from Langbro"
(a mental institution). But whether she is crazy or not, there
is so much misery among these wrecks of humanity that her
protest does not matter. Some lie in their beds and vacantly
stare at the ceiling, bloated and deformed by their ailments,
while others are mere skeletons, with their skin drawn tightly
like parchment over their protruding bones. All are awaiting
death, for these corridors lead only to the grave.

There are only two resident physicians for all the 800 patients, while two others make occasional calls. And there are
only twenty nurses. I asked Dr. Sven Lindquist, one of the
resident doctors, whether he did not find it depressing to
work in such a place, but he said he liked the work because
the old people were so grateful for what little he could do for
them.

Harry Biltberg, the aging superintendent of Rosenlund
who conducted me through the institution, is the authority
for the statement that over 300 patients die a year—an average of almost one a day. There is a combined chapel and

entertainment room with the morgue directly behind it. It is a cold, gloomy room with long, narrow windows. At the far end of it is an altar with candlesticks on each side. In the center is a religious picture—a ship at sea in a storm, heading towards a beacon in the shape of the Cross. Church services are held here on Sundays. And twice a week the hall is transformed into an entertainment room. A curtain is drawn across the altar and a movie screen is pulled down over the central picture. There are movies and an occasional musical performance.

Gossip travels quickly among the idle, and word has got around that an American is visiting the institution. At the end of my visit, a nurse informs me that an old man who has relatives in America is anxious to talk to me. I meet him in a waiting room. He is a handsome old man with a long white mustache, wearing an open shirt, a blue coat, and bed-room slippers. He would like me to bring greetings to his two daughters in the United States, but he cannot remember their married names or where they live. He fumbles in his back pocket for a well-worn wallet. Slowly he goes through a sheaf of papers. At last he finds an old yellow slip with the names and addresses. I promise to write and tell them about him. He would like to have a word from them before he dies, and he has not heard from them in years. I have written to the two daughters in Brooklyn, but I have not had any word either.

It is these conditions at Rosenlund and in some of the older institutions that have brought such a loud protest from Ivar Lo-Johansson and have been the subject of his bestsellers. His revelations and criticism have stirred wide controversy. His own youthful experience brought him into intimate contact with the old-age problem. The son of a poor tenant farmer, he relates how he was obliged to take his own mother to an old-age home, where she died three months later of a broken heart. "I left her with flowers in the window," he writes, "and with the promise that she would return home by summer, but we both knew that this would never be. Although she pretended she was happy, she lost the will to live. Her death in the old-age home, like so many other members of my family, left a very bitter memory. She had gone there to relieve me of the burden of looking after her and I knew that it was partly my fault."

In his book *The Illiterate*, which was autobiographical, Ivar Lo-Johansson tells of several instances in which elderly people were forced into old-age homes against their will. He recalls in particular how his uncle Janne, for whom he had great respect and affection, was forcibly removed to an old-age home. Uncle Janne was a small farmer who had accumulated some capital, but the local welfare authorities felt he was "living beneath his level." They considered his behavior strange because he carried his money around with him instead of placing it in a bank and they accused him of being a "danger to the community." When the police came to lead Janne away, he could not understand what it was all about. Because he resisted violently he was considered insane and placed in solitary confinement. Eventually he became insane and died in the old people's home.

Against this background, Ivar Lo-Johansson has waged a campaign, in his writings and over the radio, to keep the aged out of old people's homes. He argues that they should be sent to institutions only when they are sick or chronically ill, mentally or physically. The old-age homes, he says, should be like hospitals, and the aged should have the prospect of being able to recover instead of contemplating only death. The healthy aged, he feels, should be kept in their homes, and if they are unable to look after themselves, paid social workers should help them out. This is being done in a very limited way now, but Ivar Lo-Johansson estimates that some

50,000 household helpers would be needed. He believes this would cost the Government and the municipalities less than building large numbers of old-age institutions.

Ivar Lo-Johansson condemns the mixing of the healthy and the insane, as is the case in many institutions in the country in Sweden. He says, "People who have worked hard all their lives deserve a better fate than to spend the remainder of their days with imbeciles, epileptics, and the chronically ill." Love and work, he contends, are the two elements lacking in the old-age homes. Love is frowned upon, he says, and marriages are generally forbidden, while the aged, removed from their own surroundings, have nothing to do but wait in boredom for the end. He calls the old-age homes "concentration camps" and refers to the inmates as the "gray Negroes" of Sweden.

Welfare officials agree with some of Ivar Lo-Johansson's arguments, but they contend that he is fanatical. There was a time when old people were forced into old-age homes when they were considered no longer capable of looking after themselves, but such cases are rare now. There is only half enough space in the old-age homes for those who actually need care, and since every Swede receives a State pension and there is a limited possibility of supplying social workers in the home, there is less reason to remove the aged to institutions. Authorities point out that Ivar Lo-Johansson's suggestion for an army of household workers to help the aged is impractical because there is a shortage of labor in Sweden and there is no chance of recruiting any large number of helpers. They admit, however, that the healthy, sick, and mentally ill are mixed in many old people's homes, but this is due to lack of space, a condition which they are trying to remedy as quickly as possible by new building.

It is actually the policy of the Government to keep as many old people in their own homes as possible. This is regarded as the best place for them so long as they are able to care for themselves. The vast majority of the aged dread the idea of entering an old people's home. They believe a certain shame attaches to it. They feel they will be deprived of their freedom, and they do not want to forsake their own surroundings, however humble. They think entering a home severs their last tie with the living world and is a one-way street to the grave. Figures show that only 6 per cent of the aged in Sweden are in institutions. The remainder are, for the most part, in their own homes and looking after themselves as best they can. Of a total of 635,000 persons over sixty-seven years of age, it is estimated that 420,000—two-thirds—are completely dependent upon the State pension and the housing and other supplements.

Mr. and Mrs. Karl Johan Svensson provide a typical example of an old-age couple completely dependent upon State and municipal benefits for their support. They live in the southern part of Stockholm in a poorer section, but it has nothing in common with slums. Like many other old people, the Svenssons do not understand much about their finances. All they know is that they receive a total of 410 crowns a month ($82) in benefits. This includes the basic old-age pension for both of them and the extras for housing, heating, and an allowance for the cost of living.

Svensson, who is seventy-seven years old, was a tenant farmer in his earlier days but he made no more than a bare living. Thirty years ago he moved to Stockholm and was employed in a stable. The Svenssons were handicapped by a large family of nine children to raise—seven girls and two boys. Eight of them are now married and live in or near Stockholm, while the unmarried daughter is working as a servant in England. None of them is wealthy, but the men of the family earn enough as laborers or mechanics so that the women do not have to work, other than to look after their own households. There are over a score of grandchildren.

The Svenssons have had a hard life with never a cent to spare. Mrs. Svensson says she does not know how they came through it all. "I cried and prayed and we managed somehow," she relates. Now with their State pension and benefits, they are in better circumstances than they have ever been. But Mrs. Svensson's motto still is: "Never buy anything at the beginning of the month that you would not buy at the end of it." They have a two-room apartment with kitchen, but there is no bathroom and the heating is by means of an old-fashioned porcelain stove, common in the Swedish countryside. They rent out one room to a worker and have to cross his room to reach theirs.

When I first met the Svenssons they were satisfied and felt they could continue on their own. But since then adversity has struck. Mrs. Svensson has suffered a stroke and is in hospital, and her husband, left to his own devices, is having trouble with small chores such as buying food, cooking, and doing laundry. He is also bewildered by the tragedy of finding himself alone. But he is determined to avoid being taken to an old-age home no matter what happens. None of the eight married children have come forward to lend a helping hand, but Svensson remarks philosophically that they have their own lives to lead. They seem to consider that it is not their responsibility to look after their parents so long as the welfare state provides for them. This is a very general attitude and is another target of Ivar Lo-Johansson, who complains that Sweden is "overorganized and overinstitutionalized" and remarks sadly that "a mother can take care of many children, but many children cannot take care of a mother."

The program for the care of the aged in Sweden gained momentum after World War II. It is since then that the

pension law has been passed and that the new model homes
for the aged have been built. In the early part of the century
progress was slow while the social program was in its forma-
tive stage. It came almost to a standstill during the uncertain
war years when Sweden was virtually blockaded and the
shortages made new building impossible. The span from
Rosenlund to Sabbatsberg illustrates what has taken place
over sixty-five years, but Sweden is still far from its goal and
there are many more Rosenlunds than there are Sabbats-
bergs. The ratio is approximately four to one. The main objective, in the future, is to provide every inmate of an old-age
institution with his own room. Ernst Bexelius, head of the
Social Welfare Board, estimates that it will take from twenty
to thirty years to accomplish this. It would eliminate, at least
in part, what Ali Berggren, chief inspector of old-age homes,
considers to be the darkest spot in Sweden's welfare program,
for it would put an end to the mixture of sane and insane,
sick and healthy, in such close proximity.

Berggren agrees to a certain extent with Ivar Lo-Johansson. He believes that the sick among the aged should be sent
to hospitals, like anyone else, and that they do no belong
in old-age institutions. When they recover, he feels they
should be returned to their homes if they are able to look
after themselves. Only those who cannot should be placed in
old-age homes. He estimates that 10 per cent of the aged are
sick and should be hospitalized, that another 10 per cent
should be in old-age homes, but that the remainder should
be left in their own homes to lead as normal a life as possible. If Berggren has his way there will be no more model
homes such as Sabbatsberg or even settlements such as
Nockeby. He feels that the inmates of Sabbatsberg are well
enough to look after themselves and should not be in any
kind of institution, and he is against the segregation of the
aged in a settlement. He would provide homes or apartments

for them in communities where they are mixed with younger people so that they may continue to have a normal existence and retain the will to live and the incentive to work if possible.

Berggren wants twice as many homes for the aged as now exist, but he wants smaller institutions which would accommodate from twenty to thirty persons so that they would receive more individual care, and he wants these homes located near communities so that the inmates can continue to maintain contact with the life around them. He would have the sick removed from these institutions and cared for in hospitals.

No one has yet provided a solution to relieve the dreadful monotony of the old-age institutions. An effort is being made in some of them to provide the patients with handicraft work, but this fails to supply the mental stimulus for people who may be physically handicapped but still retain a clear mind. Many lapse into complete inertia in which the will to live is no more than an instinct.

The care of the aged in Sweden is reaching toward a technical perfection probably unmatched anywhere. But whether it be in Sabbatsberg or Nockeby or any of the other modern institutions, there is one element lacking—there is no warmth. These long corridors with their bright, shiny linoleum surfaces reverberate with the hollow sound of one's own voice and footsteps, where voices never rise above a whisper and footsteps are no more than a muffled shuffle. There is no laughter here, no merriment, no little children to rend the air with their cries of joy or even with their tears. There is only silence—the silence of utter boredom. These are things which the welfare state, however benevolent, cannot provide. The feeling is inescapable that many of these old people would far prefer a life of poverty among their own loved ones than this clean, orderly, perfected existence in model institutions.

It can well be argued that the youth of today has no time for the aged. The pattern of life has changed. A century ago, 80 per cent of Sweden's population lived on the farm, which was a family business in which old and young took part. Now only 60 per cent of the people are engaged in agriculture, and another million have been absorbed into industry and have to punch a time clock away from home. The pace of life has quickened and many of the younger people feel they cannot shoulder the responsibility in caring for the aged. They have their own children to raise and they want to bring them up in their own way. The gap between generations is too wide. These are valid reasons, but they are undoubtedly coupled with too willing a disposition to accept the State's responsibility in place of their own. There are too many children like those of Karl Johan Svensson. The pattern of the future is one of mechanical perfection, but without the heartbeat that only the people can give to it.

CHAPTER XI

Prison Reform

SWEDEN is probably the world's most progressive country in prison care and reform. Special attention is given to the welfare of a prisoner so as not to breed resentment in him and to fit him to resume his place in society after he has served his punishment. A new prison law of 1946 declares that a prisoner shall be treated with firmness and earnestness "but with respect for his dignity as a human being."

The leniency shown toward prisoners is amazing to any foreigner who acquires a knowledge of the Swedish penal system and might well surprise many Swedes who are unfamiliar with it. Capital punishment was abolished in 1921, and there have been no executions for over forty years. Most prisoners are granted leave from prison at intervals; they are occasionally permitted to work outside of prison if they have a special skill and can be trusted, or if they are nearing the end of their sentence so as to prepare them for renewed contact with the outside world; and murderers are frequently committed to mental institutions and released after a brief period.

There has been a controversy for the past twenty years between the progressives who advocate increased leniency—having in mind particularly the welfare of the individual criminal—and the more conservative element, which fears the consequences to society of this leniency and which points, with justification, to the increasing crime figures in recent years. Statistics show that crime has increased 50 per cent in Sweden within the past five years, and this is a hard argument to combat.

The progressives have had the upper hand, and all recent legislation has been molded to their way of thinking. In the eyes of the law, loss of freedom is regarded as such a punishment in itself that there is no need for "further severity," and a very great measure of discretion is given to the courts in the interpretation of the law and to superintendents of prisons and prison boards in administering punishment. The objective is clearly set forth in the prison law, which states that it is the duty of a prison official "to put a prisoner on his feet and not to become an agent for the vengeful sentiments of the least enlightened members of society." Helen Lindahl, daughter of a prosecutor who has made a study of prison care, explains it this way: "The prisoner is given to understand that he has a chance to make a new life for himself and again become a valuable member of society. Leniency is not quite the right word, since we do not intend to be lenient in the sense that implies a disregard for justice and society. We are aiming at a system which is morally and socially right for the individual, and it may appear mild in comparison with the older system when only punishment was considered."

Einar Ljungberg, who once served a term for lese majesty and who is now an active prison reformer, says, "Imprisonment must not be a matter of revenge, but we must think of making good citizens out of our prisoners. We should show confidence in them. If they misuse it they should be deprived of it, but everyone is entitled to it."

The Swedish prison law contends that since society is protected so long as an offender is confined in prison, there is nothing to be gained by treating a prisoner harshly. A report of the Penal Code Commission declared that "it is impossible to turn an offender into a law-abiding and decent member of society by creating in him a rebellion against its methods of disciplining him, or by preparing him for a parasitic life after his release by removing from him all opportunities for initiative and the development of social responsibility." Prison officials are called upon, on the contrary, "to make conditions in prison resemble life in a free society in so far as possible and encourage the prisoner's efforts and capacity for independent work."

Leniency applies to the system as a whole. In 1954, there was an average of 2,900 men in prison in Sweden and 70 women out of a population of 7,200,000. This is an extremely low figure. Sweden is an orderly country and there is relatively little crime. There is a general prosperity and a high standard of living, circumstances which mitigate against crime. Such offenses as do occur are largely the result of drunkenness or personal and family quarrels, and there is no organized crime. But this does not in itself explain the small number of prisoners. It is, in large part, the result of letting off first offenders and those who commit minor crimes with fines or suspended sentences. Only one male offender in four goes to jail, and only one woman offender in twenty-five ever serves a prison term. The law now provides for a suspended sentence for a first offender who commits any crime which calls for a penalty of no more than two years' imprisonment. Over 8,000 suspended sentences were handed down by the Swedish courts last year.

Greater leniency is shown toward women than toward

men. This will be denied by some judicial and legal authorities, who will contend that the laws are administered equally irrespective of sex, but the figures speak for themselves. Women commit 15 per cent of the crimes committed in Sweden, yet women prisoners account for less than 3 per cent of those serving jail sentences. Torsten Eriksson, a top official of the Ministry of Justice, says that this is "chivalry," but Swedish feminists explain it otherwise. Miss Valborg Lundgren, a prominent woman lawyer, contends that women commit relatively minor offenses, mostly sex crimes which go unpunished although the law provides punishment. She explains that the courts feel that no good purpose is served by imposing sentences and "ruining people's lives unnecessarily."

Statistics show that few women commit a second offense, and this is considered evidence in support of the system of handing down suspended sentences. In such cases a supervisor is appointed for a probationary period to see that the offender leads a good life and does not return to crime. If the supervisor is not satisfied that his ward intends to reform, the suspended sentence may be revoked and the offender compelled to serve a prison term, but such cases are extremely rare.

Virtually every prisoner who has served more than six months in jail obtains a full three days' leave from prison four times a year, a total of at least twelve days outside of the institution. Extra leave may also be granted to visit a near relative who is seriously ill, to attend a relative's funeral, or for some important personal or family reason. The prisoner is supplied with regular clothes and is released without supervision. There is nothing to indicate that he is a prisoner, so that he may feel entirely free during his leave period. Lifetime prisoners are given the same leave privileges, but must obtain the permission of the Prison Board. Leaves are granted in all cases where "no danger of abuse is assumed to exist," and that is the general assumption unless proved otherwise. Prison officials contend that the system has worked satisfactorily and point out that only 2 per cent of prisoners thus released have failed to return or have committed minor offenses during their absence from prison. They believe the system is useful in restoring a prisoner's self-confidence, in preparing him for eventual release from prison, and that it provides a solution to the sexual problem. There is little difficulty in a small country such as Sweden in rounding up prisoners who fail to return. There are penalties for those who violate their leave, including an extension of the jail sentence or cancellation of future leave, and this, in most cases, is a sufficient deterrent.

Prisoners are encouraged to keep up their family ties while in jail. This is done in the belief that it is generally a better influence than association with other prisoners outside of jail. Leave is granted more frequently and more easily to those who have families close at hand.

Prison sentences are automatically shortened. Prisoners who serve more than a six-month sentence have it reduced by one-sixth, but it may be cut by as much as a third for good behavior. Some supervision outside of prison is maintained during the remainder of the term. Prisoners who are nearing the end of their sentence are occasionally provided with jobs outside of prison if they have a particular skill; they leave jail in the morning and return to sleep at night.

Although the number of prisoners in Sweden is small, it is divided among some fifty prisons. It is felt that a large concentration of prisoners in a single institution presents a danger of unrest, since it is difficult to prevent unfavorable associations, and that the smaller prisons offer more chance for individual care and supervision. This is probably one of the reasons why there have been no prison riots in Sweden.

There are approximately thirty walled institutions and twenty open ones where prisoners are employed as laborers in agriculture and forestry. These are more like camps, and prisoners wander out over the fields and in the forests without guards. Prisons do not serve a particular locality, but are intended to care for a certain type of prisoner according to a selective system which carefully investigates his background and the circumstances of his crime. The largest prison in Sweden is Långholmen Prison in Stockholm, which houses 500 of the worst offenders. But here, too, a distinction is made. The more hardened criminals are kept behind bars, while lesser offenders, or those who show a greater desire to reform, are assigned to quarters in the outer buildings where there is more freedom.

Prisoners never die in prison unless it is a sudden death. If they are considered so sick that their recovery is unlikely, they are removed to a hospital outside of prison so they may end their days in freedom. Women are also taken to a hospital outside of prison at the time of childbirth so that the child may escape a stigma which might remain for life.

The physician is called upon to play an increasing role in the penal system. Every prisoner is given a medical examination, with particular emphasis on his mental condition. This is especially important in cases of murder, and murderers are rarely sent to jail. They are instead committed to mental institutions from which they may be discharged when they are no longer considered a danger to society. This is the result of a liberal interpretation of two famous clauses in the penal law, known as 5:5 and 5:6. Under Chapter 5, Article 5, no one may be convicted for a crime committed while he is suffering from "insanity, mental debility, or any other mental abnormality that may be considered tantamount to insanity." Article 6 goes further and exempts from punishment any person who commits a crime in a "temporary state of insanity." It is provided that such criminals be kept in "security" in a mental institution. This opens the way for a great many criminals, particularly murderers, to escape long prison terms, and lawyers invariably claim that their clients are what are called "five-fivers" or "five-sixers."

But even more extraordinary is a further provision, under the same Article 6, to the effect that crimes committed under "temporary insanity" shall, in certain cases, be given a sentence "milder than the minimum punishment provided by law." This is also meant to cover crimes committed under the influence of liquor and has become one of the most debated points in the penal law. Criminals who come within the interpretation of this provision are sent to alcoholic homes or mental institutions until they are cured. The intent of the law seems to be that this clause shall apply to alcoholics and not to occasional drunks. It is contended that a person may be rendered temporarily insane by habitual drinking, but that the law is not designed to enable someone to consume a bottle of liquor, commit a crime, and escape with a mild punishment. The Supreme Court has ruled that the law is intended to cover "pathological but not normal intoxication," but obviously it is difficult to draw the line. That is left to the medical authorities and to the courts, which rely heavily upon medical advice.

Opinions on this controversial clause are many and varied, but one prominent judicial authority explained it to me as follows: "A criminal found to be insane falls within the provisions of articles 5:5 or 5:6 of the penal law regardless of whether his insanity has been brought on by alcoholism or some other cause. A mere acute intoxication cannot be considered an extenuating circumstance. Whether a criminal is sane or insane is purely a medical question for the doctors to determine."

Even criminals who are imprisoned may later be found by

the prison physician to be suffering from a mental abnormality and transferred to a mental institution from which they may gain an early release. There is the well-known case of Sven Teodor Engström, convicted as a spy during World War II for having sold plans of Sweden's northern defense line to the Russians. He was sentenced to life imprisonment, but when he had served five years in jail, the prison physician found that he was a mental case and he was sent to a mental institution from which he was freed in a short time.

There are now eleven men serving lifetime sentences in Sweden, including eight murderers and three spies. There are no women serving life terms and there have been none for the past quarter of a century. At the same time, there are some 500 criminals tucked away in mental or alcoholic institutions waiting to be pronounced cured and to regain their freedom. The case of the Stockholm streetcar conductor who murdered his girl friend and is now employed as a clerk of the court in a small town provides a spectacular example of the process of rehabilitation which the present Swedish penal system aims at.

The crime occurred six years ago and the name of the streetcar conductor is unknown except to intimates. Swedish authorities go to great lengths to conceal the names of such criminals because, as one official explained to me, "It would harm the offender and make it difficult for him to create a new life for himself." The streetcar conductor shot his girl friend in her apartment, surrendered to the police, and admitted the murder. He was found to have been in an abnormal state of mind when he committed the crime and he was therefore sent to a mental institution from which he was released less than a year later.

During his time in hospital, the enterprising streetcar conductor devoted himself to studying law, and two years after his release he obtained a law degree. He then applied and was accepted as an assistant clerk of the court in a small town where he was unknown. All went well until a Stockholm newspaper learned of his appointment and his record became public. As a result, his appointment to the court was suspended. The Court of Appeals, before which his case was taken, recommended that he be given a new mental examination. This was not done, however, but instead his case was brought up before the King in Council, the highest authority in the land, consisting of the King and members of his cabinet. His appointment was approved and he was reinstated.

Six months later, the former streetcar conductor was in line for promotion to clerk of the court and this again stirred up the whole matter. The Court of Appeals decided on this second occasion, however, that since the King in Council had approved his reinstatement and he seemed qualified to fill the position of clerk, it could not do otherwise than approve his appointment. In handing down this decision which has set a precedent, the President of the court declared, "We hope that this man will now be accepted back in society, but I must stress that this decision was taken with the greatest hesitation and not without reluctance."

One of the most remarkable examples of leniency, or what is considered in Sweden to be humane treatment of a prisoner, is the case of Bror Erik Hedström, one of five members of the so-called Sala League, the only organized criminal gang in Sweden in this century. The gang, which operated in the thirties, was responsible for a series of murders and robberies and was led by Sigvard Thuneman, the master mind, who is said to have exerted a hypnotic influence over the others and who is now confined to a mental institution for "life." Thuneman, however, has been given an opportunity to study languages and is now specializing in Sanskrit and Arabic and doing translation work for Uppsala University.

Hedström was closest to Thuneman. He was charged with

murder, robbery, arson, and the theft of eight cars. He was sentenced to two lifetime terms, plus nine years and eight months' imprisonment. There was every reason to believe that he would never live to be free again. He began serving his sentence in Långholmen Prison in Stockholm on July 2, 1937. Hedström had been a laborer but had an interest in mechanics, and he was assigned, in prison, to the mechanical workshop. He was paid a wage of from sixty to eighty cents a day, which was double the wage received by other prisoners employed in less skilled work. In this way, Hedström was able to accumulate a small amount of money.

Hedström experimented and he developed a new type of screw that would withstand vibration. He was encouraged in his work by the prison authorities, who helped him with data and supplied him with the necessary tools to carry on with his invention. In February, 1945, less than eight years after his imprisonment, he was allowed to take a job outside of prison with a well-known engineering firm in Stockholm and was paid a regular salary. He turned this money over to the prison authorities, who deducted thirty cents a day for his board and lodging in prison and remitted the balance to his family. Hedström left the prison at seven o'clock every morning and, as his place of employment was far away, he did not return until seven-thirty at night. He used his savings to pay for streetcar fare and meals outside of prison.

Shortly after Hedström was jailed, presumably for life, his wife divorced him. After he obtained the job outside of prison, he renewed his contact with his family and occasionally lunched with his wife and children, who were kept in ignorance of his past and did not know their father was a prisoner.

A year later, Hedström filed a petition for pardon and the prison authorities recommended that it be granted despite the serious nature of the crimes for which he was imprisoned, on the ground that he had shown "laudable energy in re-habilitating himself during his imprisonment." Pardon was granted mainly because of his renewed contact with his family which, it was felt, gave promise that he seriously meant to reform. Upon his release, after serving only nine years, he remarried his former wife and the prison authorities raised a fund of $200 as a wedding present toward refurnishing his home. He was released on five years' probation, during which he was under the care of a supervisor. Hedström is now a free man and is employed by a large engineering firm, but his past is unknown to his factory colleagues.

While judicial authorities believe prisoners should be accepted back into society once they have served their punishment, the public is not so liberal-minded and does not easily accept them either at work or socially. There have been cases of strikes among workers when it has been discovered that a former prisoner was employed. The prison authorities have frequently petitioned the King to allow a prisoner to change his name in cases where criminals were well-known because of publicity they had received. It is easier in Sweden, however, for an ex-convict to conceal his past, even in a small town, because there is less curiosity about other people's business than exists, for instance, in the United States. This is not to say that there is no gossip in the smaller communities, but Swedes hold to the belief that a man's business is his own concern, and this enables a great deal of freedom of behavior.

A remarkable clause in the Swedish penal law absolves from punishment a person who, in the course of committing a crime, voluntarily changes his mind and does not go through with it. This provision was recently put to its first test in a sensational case which so closely duplicated the circumstances of *An American Tragedy*, by Theodore Dreiser, that the man involved was believed to have obtained his idea from the famous American novel or from the movie *A Place in the Sun,* then showing in Sweden.

It all happened on a summer's night. Sten Sundberg, a thirty-five-year-old caretaker, had just been told by his girl friend that she was expecting a child. Unknown to her at the time, Sundberg was already the father of three illegitimate children by two other women and was having difficulty supporting them on his small salary. The girl said she could arrange to have a legal abortion but she preferred to keep the child and wanted him to marry her so that the child would be legitimate. Sundberg flew into a rage and insisted that the girl go through with the abortion, but he suggested that they talk the matter over further and proposed to take her for a boat ride on the following evening. He persuaded her to bring her bicycle along on the outing.

He picked her up with his motorboat the next evening at a deserted place in the Stockholm archipelago and took her bicycle aboard. They argued for hours about the child until she grew tired and retired to the cabin below deck for a rest. She undressed, got into a sleeping bag, and went to sleep. She was suddenly awakened at midnight when a flashlight was turned on her and Sundberg called to her to run up on deck to help disentangle the propeller, which he said had got caught in some of the rigging. She looked for her clothes but could not find them; running up to the deck naked, she saw nothing wrong with the boat. According to her account, Sundberg picked her up, kissed her, and threw her overboard. When she came to the surface in the icy water, the motorboat was speeding away. But it soon came back and headed directly for her, ramming her two or three times.

After a while she was able to catch on to the dinghy, but when Sundberg realized that she was hanging on, he headed out across the bay at full speed. She shouted to him but he paid no attention. The girl claims that he only lifted her out of the water when other boats were nearing and he became frightened. When he finally took her aboard, her watch had stopped, showing she had been in the water for forty-five minutes. When she asked him whether he had tried to murder her, he replied that it was just a joke.

As the result of her experience, the girl suffered a miscarriage and was hospitalized for several weeks. She told the story to the doctor and to some intimate friends, and when her father heard about it, he notified the police. In the meantime, Sundberg tried to persuade her to write a statement that she had fallen in the water from her bicycle. It was brought out during the trial that Sundberg had hidden her clothing while she was asleep and the prosecutor intimated that the man had planned, if she had drowned, to leave her bicycle along the shore and scatter her clothing near by to give the impression that she had drowned accidentally while out for a swim.

There were no witnesses to the drama. The court had only the stories of the girl and the man to go by. But the girl told her story with conviction, while the man changed his version repeatedly. He contended that the girl had fallen into the water accidentally and that he had circled around her in the dark in an attempt to pick her up. As for the rest, he pleaded nervousness and inability to remember the events. The girl's name has never appeared in print nor have any pictures of her, since Swedish law protects her from any publicity that would harm her reputation. In court, however, she was referred to as Birgit.

In court the girl, a sandy blonde in her early twenties, appeared fresh and frail. She was not the athletic type who might have been expected to survive such an experience by her own efforts. She told her story with obvious reluctance and appeared to be still in love with the man, in spite of all that had happened. Sundberg, a strong, rough-looking type with sharply cut features and dark wavy hair, sat impassive.

It was evident from the outset of the trial that the aged

jury of three women and six men who sat on the bench with the judge believed the girl's story and had no faith in the man's evasive and confused answers. The prosecutor claimed that Sundberg had made no less than three attempts to murder the girl: when he threw her into the water, when he rammed her with the boat, and when he dragged her behind it across the bay.

Sundberg's attorney, Ragnar Gottfarb, one of Sweden's cleverest criminal lawyers, was hesitant at first to base his case entirely on the new provision of law which would have freed his client from punishment in case of a voluntary change of mind, since this called for an admission that Sundberg meant to murder the girl. He first made the usual plea that his client was in an abnormal state of mind. Even the prosecutor joined him in asking for a mental examination of the defendant. It was only after Sundberg had been pronounced sane and not in need of treatment in a mental institution that Gottfarb returned to argue that if the court found that Sundberg meant to murder the girl, he had voluntarily changed his mind since he had pulled her out of the water and saved her life. Gottfarb asked, "Who can say what was in the man's mind at the moment?"

After four hours' deliberation with the members of the jury, Justice Bengt Sandegren returned with the verdict. He read the concise statement in a low but authoritative tone in an atmosphere of tense solemnity. The court, he said, rejected the idea that Sundberg had undergone a voluntary change of mind and had concluded that he pulled Birgit out of the water only when he was frightened of being observed. The court therefore found Sundberg guilty of premeditated attempted murder. The sentence—ten years' imprisonment.

The girl crumpled in a heap over her desk, sobbing convulsively, while Sundberg heard his fate without flexing a muscle and with the same stony indifference he had shown throughout the trial. The spectators filed slowly out of the courtroom and the curtain was rung down on "the Swedish Tragedy." Since then both the Court of Appeals and the Supreme Court have upheld the sentence, but with good behavior Sundberg may be free in six or seven years.

Some startling proposals have been made for revision of the present penal law which, if approved by Parliament, would come into effect this year. After a study extending over sixteen years, a special commission headed by Birger Ekeberg, Grand Marshal of the royal household, one of Sweden's most distinguished jurists, has recommended that "mercy killing" be permitted by a relative of a dying person to shorten his suffering, but not by a doctor.

According to the commission's report, if a dying person asks a relative to shorten his life, the latter may in such a case be given less punishment than he would for manslaughter and may be totally exempt from punishment in exceptional cases. The commission, for instance, felt that manslaughter would be too severe a charge in a case where parents killed a physically or mentally defective child to save it from prolonged suffering. The report made it clear, however, that this right is not to be extended to doctors, since "it might seriously impair public confidence in their treatment of the sick." It declared:

"There has been serious discussion both in this country and abroad as to whether a physician should have the right to shorten the suffering of a hopelessly sick patient by painlessly advancing his death. This question has been discussed by the commission but it has refrained from any special ruling. However carefully such a ruling might be framed, it might be expected to lead to misunderstanding and to rumors that the lives of patients in hospitals were not safe. With regard to such cases, the commission has adhered to the normal punishment. There are exceptional cases, but they are so few that no general stipulations are required."

The commission reported that it had also considered the

possibility of freeing a relative from punishment for mercy killing when the dying person did not request it, but this was rejected because it would give rise to "misunderstanding and misuse."

Another proposal would reduce a charge of murder to that of manslaughter if a person who was maltreated or subjected to severe mental pressure for a prolonged period of time eventually killed his persecutor. This has been interpreted as meaning that a man who, for instance, was tormented by his mother-in-law and murdered her to escape continued persecution would only be guilty of manslaughter and not of murder. Yet another debatable clause provides that rape "may apply within marriage," but it is left to the discretion of the public prosecutor to decide whether to bring such a case into court.

One of the biggest problems facing judicial authorities in Sweden is the care of juvenile delinquents. Crime has increased enormously among the youth, and one out of every three crimes is now committed by delinquents under twenty-one years of age. They are treated even more leniently than adults, reform of the individual being even more important for the rising generation.

Since there are no juvenile courts in Sweden, delinquents are handled either by the Child Welfare Board or by the regular courts, or by both working together. They fall into three age groups: those under fifteen; those between fifteen and eighteen; and those between eighteen and twenty-one. There are definite limits to the penalties for each group, although a great deal of discretion is given to the authorities in handling individual cases. Those under fifteen years of age are dealt with exclusively by the Child Welfare Board and, for the most part, are exempt from punishment. Those in the middle group may not be sentenced to prison, but the worst offenders may be sent to reformatories. Lesser offenders are dealt with by the Child Welfare Board, which may order a change of environment, send them to vocational schools, place them under supervision, or dismiss them with a mere warning. The older group, between eighteen and twenty-one, is treated somewhat less mildly, and the worst offenders may be sent to jail or at least to a reformatory. But most are given a suspended sentence under supervision or are freed with the customary warning.

Whatever the law and its theoretical application, in practice the vast majority of youthful delinquents is placed under supervision or set free. There are not more than 200 juvenile delinquents in reformatories in Sweden, but there are thousands at liberty under some form of supervision. The greatest stress is placed on this supervision because it is expected to exert the reforming influence. But judging from the increase in juvenile crimes, the system has been a failure. The idealistic approach has not yielded the results that were expected of it. The delinquents have shown that they are much more hardened than the optimistic social and welfare workers ever believed them to be. Torsten Eriksson, who has made a special study of crime recurrence among youth, has found that three-quarters of the offenders who have been dealt with have returned to crime. The old stern method of imprisonment, he says, was a failure. Youth prisons have also been a failure. But leniency has not supplied the answer either.

When a youth commits a crime, the procedure is a somewhat complex one. He is arrested and brought to the local police station, where he is questioned. This inquiry does not deal only with the crime: the offender's background is meticulously examined. He is then released, and the report is forwarded to the district attorney. This may take weeks or even months. In the meantime, the report is carefully checked. The district attorney determines the handling of the case. If the offender is under eighteen years of age, there is a possibility that he may not be prosecuted at all. Otherwise, the case will be referred either to the Child Welfare Board or to the court in the event that the offense is a grave one. There is no clear line of demarcation between the Child Welfare Board and the court. Both have an equal right to deal with the case, and they frequently do, though not always without conflict. If there is a difference of opinion as to how the offender should be treated, the more severe penalty applies.

One of the most common offenses among juvenile delinquents is the theft of cars. But this is known, under Swedish law, as "borrowing" and not theft because the cars are not kept or resold but are taken mostly for pleasure. The culprits may want a joy ride, or they may be anxious to try out a new model car, or they may merely be seeking excitement. Invariably the cars are abandoned after a short ride, or at least when the gasoline runs out. This is regarded as a minor crime and most offenders are let off with no more than a suspended sentence, even for repeated offenses. A suspended sentence is mandatory in the case of a first offense, and delinquents with a record behind them frequently take advantage of this and urge others who have no backlog of crime to do the "borrowing." The extreme leniency with regard to car theft is no doubt responsible for the fact that one car in every twenty was "borrowed" last year.

But if the theft of cars is treated lightly, driving under the influence of liquor is regarded as a serious offense, and no leniency is shown either adults or juveniles. Any driver who is suspected of drunken driving may be stopped by the police and a blood test taken. If the test shows that there is more than a certain percentage of alcohol in the blood, the offender will be fined or sent to jail. This alternative is determined by the precise amount of alcohol revealed in the test. And there are no suspended sentences. It is figured that a small glass of Swedish schnapps (aqua vitae) consumed two hours before driving is the limit. That is why many Swedes refrain from drinking at parties if they are going to drive home. A Stockholm restaurant which specializes in good wines and liquors advertises that it will drive its clients home.

Swedish authorities are particularly concerned about the growth of juvenile delinquency because there are indications that it may be, at least in part, the result of conditions that are peculiar to the welfare state. The riots which occurred during successive summers between 1951 and 1954, in which a younger delinquent element played the dominant role, were an ugly symptom never convincingly explained. There was no apparent reason for these disturbances.

The riots occurred on Saturday nights when crowds on their way home from the movies and a popular amusement park gathered in one of the city's main squares and stood around, apparently waiting for something to happen. When the police tried to disperse the mob, there were clashes, and the spectators sided with the agitators.

During the first riots in 1951, the police were cautious, not wanting to provoke trouble, but when it became apparent that the riots were not to be broken up by mere persuasion, the police adopted sterner methods. Mounted police were used to push away the crowds, police dogs were let loose, and the police drew their swords. This angered the crowds. A policeman's sword is regarded as part of the uniform but not as a weapon, and the sight of the police swinging into action with drawn swords caused laughter and resentment. In later riots the police systematically rounded up the ringleaders. Ever since then justice officials, criminal experts, lawyers, psychiatrists, and newspapermen have been theorizing about the cause of the outbreaks.

They seem agreed on one point—that there was no political motive behind the riots. Swedish authorities reject the idea that they were Communist-inspired. Obviously the Communists would be glad to foment trouble with the police, taking advantage of the fact that the police are unpopular in a country where the people resent taking orders and are proud of their freedom. But the ringleaders had no Communist ties. They were delinquents, some with a police record and some with a prison record. The motive could not be economic either. There is too much prosperity for that. The people are well fed, well clothed, have money, and they can afford entertainment—the movies and an occasional theater. The housing shortage and overcrowding may be a reason why younger people roam the streets, but the trouble seems to have been psychological. Since there is no need to struggle for an existence, life in the welfare state has become too soft—too dull and routine. There is a lack of stimulus, and it has given rise to a craving for excitement, particularly among younger people. They riot—and they steal cars—to relieve the monotony and boredom of a good living and to satisfy a suppressed zest for adventure.

This feeling is unconsciously betrayed in a film produced by the Social Democratic Party for election purposes. The hero of the film is a young man in his early twenties who was a truck driver in West Germany. It is a scene of desolation and despair. This part of the picture was evidently taken just after the German defeat and is intended to stress the contrast with peaceful, contented Sweden. There is a political implication that Sweden did well to stay neutral. The truck driver returns home and finds conditions so perfect that he feels there is nothing more to be done. The worker's paradise is at hand and he is frustrated. Eventually he meets some old party leaders who remind him of labor's struggle over the past half-century and who point out that the battle is not quite won yet. There is still a housing shortage. He feels better and is encouraged to join the party and carry on with the program. Accidentally, the Social Democratic Party has laid its finger on one of Sweden's most difficult social problems for the future.

This state of mind may be difficult to understand outside of Sweden, and many Swedes find it hard to grasp, but it is a reality and one that is somewhat frightening because it is an entirely new phenomenon and authorities do not know how to deal with it. Justice officials believe that more leniency—although this is the trend in Sweden—is certainly not the right answer and that repressive measures will not solve the problem either. They have concluded that what is needed is more specialization in the treatment of juvenile delinquents.

As a result, a model experimental institution, known as Roxtuna, was opened last year to care for sixty-five of the worst delinquents. It consists of a cluster of small houses, with six or seven boys in each and two supervisors in constant attendance. An attempt is made to create a congenial atmosphere and at the same time to train each inmate for a trade according to his ability. Two of the houses, where the most dangerous youths are confined, are closed, but the remainder are open and there is no barricade around the compound. The staff consists of a doctor, a psychologist, a nurse, a social worker, and a number of assistants besides the supervisors—altogether fifty-one persons. The cost of maintenance is figured at as much as $22,000 per inmate. It is no wonder therefore that Parliament only gave its approval after a great deal of hesitation, for even the welfare state in its most benevolent mood cannot lightly undertake such an expenditure. Torsten Eriksson finds it justified "if it stops what might be a life-long career of crime" with grave danger to society. Roxtuna is patterned on American experience, but with the essential difference that it is intended for the worst offenders rather than the milder ones.

There are, of course, critics of the Swedish penal system and its leniency. Professor Karl Olivecrona, an authority on Swedish penal law and the prison system, argues convincingly that the stress placed upon the care of the individual prisoner overlooks the consequences to society, that crime is on the increase, and that the policy of leniency towards juvenile delinquents has been a failure. The public very largely agrees with him. A Gallup poll in which the public was asked whether it approved a jail sentence for three youthful delinquents for repeated car stealing brought out that 70 per cent approved the sentence, whereas only 20 per cent were for milder treatment. Critics contend, too, that the habit of handing down suspended sentences is greatly overdone and that criminals take every advantage of it, knowing that they will escape punishment most of the time. Lennart Asplund, a Stockholm public prosecutor, comments that if the suspended sentence led to a reduction in crime, he would be for it, but the reverse has been true.

However vocal the critics are, they will have little influence so long as the prison administration is in the hands of such progressives as Dr. Karl Schlyter, the aged but liberal chairman of the Penal Code Commission, Hardy Göransson, Director of Prisons, and Torsten Eriksson. With these men at the helm, the trend will continue toward even greater leniency. If they have their way, there will be fewer walled prisons, fewer bars and locks, and more open institutions; the prisons will be smaller and there will be more individual care and supervision; there will be more leaves for prisoners; and the prison of the future will take on increasingly the character of a reformatory or hospital for the remolding of the individual.

The quarrel is not with the stress upon the care of the individual prisoner. This is generally accepted in Sweden as desirable, but the question is how this policy can be reconciled with responsibility toward society. This feeling is well expressed by Harry Guldberg, President of Sweden's Court of Appeals, who says, "It is not really a question of reform of the individual or prevention of crime. We must have both. The idea of revenge is an ancient one rooted in primitive thinking, and individual care is more humanitarian, but society must not leave crime unpunished. It is a matter of striking a balance."

CHAPTER XII

Who Pays for the Welfare?

THE welfare program is the most expensive item in the Swedish budget. It accounts for a third of all Government, municipal, and county expenditure and exceeds the arms program, destined to protect Sweden's security and neutrality. Ernst Michanek, a leading economist in the Ministry of Social Welfare, says "social security is as much a part of our strength in international relations as the defense costs." The figures more than corroborate his statement.

The new compulsory health insurance, the cost of which cannot be definitely assessed yet, and increased old-age and children's benefits have boosted the welfare bill by more than 15 per cent within the past year. Of a total budget of $2,235,-000,000 for the fiscal year 1956-1957, about $640,000,000 goes for direct social expenditure, representing 28.6 per cent of the budget, as compared to $420,000,000 for national defense, or 18.8 per cent of the budget. When the expenses for the municipalities and county councils are added, the total cost of the welfare program amounts to approximately $1,200,-000,000, which is 16 per cent of the national income. The total cost is figured at $160 per capita.

There are no figures available regarding private contributions to the welfare program, which are limited for the most part to benefits provided by firms for their employees such as living quarters, special health and pension schemes, and recreational facilities. The tendency has been for businesses to cut down on health expenditure since the compulsory health insurance has come into effect.

The welfare program has developed mainly over the past two decades since the world depression hit Sweden in the early thirties, so that it has been a fair-weather program and has never been put to a severe test; however, Swedish economists believe that it is well adapted to meet hard times. They contend that this type of unproductive spending, to which most governments resort only in times of depression, is a guarantee of some stability, since it provides a steady income for the old-age group and some continuing help for children, no matter what the economic plight of the country might be. There could be no cut in these benefits except when there is a lowering in the cost-of-living index to which they are tied.

Gustav Holmstedt, a leading economist, says he has no illusions that a depression, particularly in the United States, would have a serious repercussion in Sweden since it would bring about a drop in exports, upon which the country's prosperity depends. But he believes that the reserve funds of the labor unions and the insurance companies would be sufficient to meet the first impact until the Government was able to put a public-works program into operation. The Government would no doubt have to trim its expenses wherever it could, but Holmstedt feels that the combined welfare and public-works programs would help Sweden back to normalcy without too much suffering. Swedish economists do not claim that their system provides an antidote to depression, but that it is well suited to withstand one if it should come.

The Government's immediate problem is to meet the increasing welfare costs. Political leaders of all shades are agreed that the saturation point has been reached as far as direct taxes are concerned. A Government committee has reached the same conclusion; since the State had to find new sources of revenue, it has turned to indirect taxation on liquor and tobacco, both Government monopolies, which together provide about half the Government's expenditure in social welfare.

The tobacco monopoly was established forty years ago, mainly to provide funds for old-age pensions, while the liquor monopoly was created at about the same time with a twofold purpose. It was set up in response to the temperance movement which exerted so much influence in the country, and it was intended in part to finance the welfare program, then in its infancy.

Conveniently enough, a special Government commission found after an eight-year study that liquor control had been a failure, and it was abolished as of October 1, 1955. In its report, the commission declared that there had been some decrease in liquor consumption when the rationing first went into effect, but it had been only temporary and the control had created a new drinking category consisting of those who felt they should acquire a ration book and use it. As a result, liquor consumption had increased considerably under the rationing system which limited purchase to persons twenty-five years of age or over and allowed heads of families from one to three quarts of hard liquor a month. Alcoholics and criminals were deprived of the right to buy liquor.

All Swedes twenty-one years of age and over may now purchase liquor from the Government stores without restrictions, and restaurants and bars may serve an unlimited amount, with the exception that drinking must be accompanied at least by a light meal and that intoxicated guests cannot be served. Since the new system has come into effect, drinking has increased 30 per cent, with an estimated increase in revenue of $60,000,000 annually. A rise in the price of tobacco is expected to bring in another $10,000,000. The increased income from both monopolies will go toward health insurance and to temperance benefits such as new homes for alcoholics.

The lifting of the liquor ban was preceded by a raise in liquor prices. A bottle of the popular Swedish schnapps, aqua vitae, which actually costs fifty cents exclusive of tax, now sells for as much as four dollars. It is evident that the Government's intention is to substitute a new form of restriction. Liquor advertising is limited to naming the brand and the price, with no praise for the product, and the Government, in conjunction with the temperance movement, is conducting a campaign to discourage excessive drinking.

The increases in the prices of liquor and tobacco have hit the laborer hardest. He is not satisfied to know that this revenue is turned into benefits, even if he receives the largest share of them. The delicate point has been reached in the balance between taxes and benefits when the average citizen has become aware that it is a matter of transferring money from one pocket to another and is asking himself whether he would not prefer to make the choice himself rather than have the Government decide for him how the money shall be spent.

Taxation has deliberately brought about a leveling of wealth, in line with Social Democratic policy, so that there are few large fortunes and incomes are limited. There are 914 millionaires (with a capital of $200,000 or more). A few of them are so wealthy and their interests so extensive that the social trend has not made a dent upon them. In this category are the Wallenberg brothers, Jacob and Marcus, famous bankers who have investments in virtually every important Swedish business enterprise. They pay the maximum income tax of 80 per cent as well as a tax on their capital assets. But Jacob Wallenberg is not worried about taxation or even the restrictions which a Social Democratic government has imposed upon the business structure; he is far more concerned about the consequences of inflation, which is sapping the savings of bank depositors.

It would be a mistake to believe that the burden of taxation falls mostly on the big industrialists and businessmen, as might be supposed. They do pay their share of the welfare program, but taxation falls on all classes, including the middle and lower salaried employees and wage earners who have few items to write off and whose savings and pensions are reduced by inflation. The middle class probably feels the pinch worst because it does not receive the same amount of benefits which are paid to the lower income group.

Lars Axelsson, head of the Taxpayers' Association, says that everyone in Sweden imagines that someone else is paying for the welfare, whereas they themselves are footing the bill. He quotes the Norwegian author Ibsen as having remarked that "the truth can live for twenty years and no longer," but he believes on the contrary that "the truth is born in twenty years and no less" and that eventually the Swedish people will wake up to the fact that the lower income groups are paying for most of the welfare and that this will put a brake on the social trend. Figures prepared by the Taxpayers' Association show that the lower income groups, with less than $2,400 a year, pay 60 per cent of the national tax bill.

There are certain peculiarities about the Swedish tax system. There is a tax on capital assets. All owners of capital in excess of $6,000 are liable to this tax. It covers all kinds of assets such as bank deposits, securities, jewelry, a car, a motorboat or sailing boat, but it does not include ordinary household effects. Certain combinations of income in conjunction with the capital tax wipe out any income from capital and sometimes exceed it. For instance, a man who earns $8,000 a year and has an income of $4,000 from capital assets is taxed $2,800 on his earnings, and he not only loses all his income from capital but owes an additional $55 in taxes. Thus it may be said that in certain circumstances a man pays to work. This, of course, discourages initiative.

Another equally discouraging factor is that husbands and wives are compelled to make a joint return, which raises both into a higher bracket and increases the tax rate. If the wife earns a substantial salary, it may prove unprofitable for her to work. For example, Mrs. Birgitta Österberg is the wife of a promising young engineer who earns approximately $5,000 a year, which is considered a fairly high salary. She has been offered a job with an advertising firm at $200 a month, but if she went to work, she would retain so small a part of her earnings that it would not cover the cost of a nursemaid to look after her two young children while she is away from home. She feels therefore that there is no point in working.

Compared with the United States, the Swedish income tax starts at a much lower figure—$240 income a year for a single person—and the tax rate is higher in the lower and middle income groups but approximately equal or less in the higher brackets. Corporation taxes are about the same as in the United States and absorb 45 per cent of the business profits of the nation.

In line with Social Democratic policy, large estates have been heavily taxed, many of them to the extent that they have had to be abandoned by their owners; at least one large estate has been confiscated outright by the Government. This was the famous castle of Bogesund, one of the most glamorous estates of the seventeenth century, which was expropriated in 1946 by special act of Parliament on the charge that its owner, Baron Nils von Höpken, had neglected the property.

Since then it has fallen even further into ruin and the grounds are now being used as a prison camp for alcoholics.

The story of Bogesund is pointed to by Swedish aristocracy as the crudest example of what socialism has done to the landed gentry. Perhaps no other estate in Sweden has had a more glorious historic past and has suffered so ignominious a fate. The famous castle was built by Per Brahe, Lord High Steward, in about 1640 during the colorful reign of Queen Christina. Per Brahe served four successive sovereigns and was rated the most powerful man in Sweden for half a century. He was one of the two most influential members of a regency council of five, appointed under the will of Charles X, successor to Christina, until the young Charles XI came of age. Per Brahe was twice governor of Finland and became Lord of Visingsö, an island in Lake Vättern in central Sweden, where he ruled "like a prince over his subjects." When the last Brahe descendant died in 1930, the family vault was locked and the key was throne into Lake Vättern as a symbol that the dynasty had come to an end.

Conveniently situated only twenty-five miles from Stockholm, Bogesund was a retreat where Per Brahe sought relaxation from affairs of state and where he entertained with a lavishness commensurate with his reputation as the wealthiest man in Sweden and in keeping with the times among the nobility. The famous warrior King Gustavus Adolphus, Queen Christina, Charles X, and Charles XI were guests at Bogesund in Per Brahe's days, a natural stopping-off place on their journeys into the countryside.

Bogesund castle was originally a quadrangular massive building of gray stone with a red brick exterior. It stood four storys high and dominated the surrounding landscape. There was a fish pond on the roof which was one of the main attractions for the distinguished guests. The walls of the castle were covered with paintings, mostly portraits of Swedish kings and noblemen. On one side of the main house were a number of bungalows for the staff, while on the other there was a beautiful garden with pavilions scattered romantically in the woods. The property included extensive hunting grounds and some farmland, but Per Brahe took only a minor interest in farming, preferring to leave nature untouched.

The castle was renovated in 1860, when it was given an entirely new face. Four square towers were built at the corners and lent the appearance of a medieval fortress. Over a period of three centuries it passed into the hands of successive noble families, more often by direct descent but sometimes also by sale. When its last owner Baron von Höpken gained possession of it, the estate consisted of approximately 1,600 acres, two-thirds of it woodland and the remainder, farmland. The castle has not been inhabited since 1916, when a fortuneteller warned von Höpken against living there.

The Government dispossessed von Höpken of Bogesund by a series of moves which left him no escape. He could not sell the estate, or any part of it, without the permission of the King, and he was given to understand that it would not be granted, while the tax was so great that he was not able to keep up the property properly. Two Government commissions were appointed to investigate von Höpken's administration of the estate. The first commission reported in 1922 that there had been no neglect and that he had tried to improve the property. A second commission in 1946 reversed the findings and declared that there was gross neglect. It was on the basis of this last report that Parliament, with a substantial Social Democratic majority, passed a special law, known as *"lex Bogesund,"* which gave the Government the authority to confiscate any estate engaged in farming if it was found that either the buildings or the farmland were neglected. Compensation was to be assessed by the Government, which paid von Höpken $2,320,000, whereas he valued Bogesund at $8,000,000. In a formal protest to Parliament, he called it robbery and charged that the expropriation was the greatest scandal ever perpetrated in Sweden.

Soon after, von Höpken died, and the proceeds, after deduction of a heavy inheritance tax, passed into the hands of young Count Stephan Wachmeister. Under the terms of the will, he is not allowed to use any of the capital, but is supposed to transmit it untouched to his heirs. Since the taxes absorb more than the total amount of the income, Wachmeister has had to appeal annually to the crown to draw on the capital. The result, he says, is that "eventually the Bogesund inheritance will be no more than a souvenir."

Today Bogesund castle is a ghost of the splendors of bygone days. A sign warns visitors not to approach its crumbling walls, painted a sickly yellow, revealing large patches of the original red brick exterior. The Brahe crest is still over the Gothic doorway and a clock near the roof is symbolically stopped at five minutes to twelve. The four corner towers with their jagged ramparts, rising high over the central building, seem menacingly poised. There is not a single windowpane left anywhere, and all the window frames are boarded up.

The prison colony is situated at the foot of a hill in the rear of the castle. There are some thirty prisoners, most of them cases of drunken driving, and they are employed in cleaning up the woods and the fields. But obviously such a small number of men can do little toward keeping up an estate which ranges far over the neighboring countryside.

Per Brahe reveled in his own glory and in that of the court and the times in which he lived. But perhaps he had a premonition of the future when he had this poem engraved on a wall of the castle:

> Let not neglect spoil
> Your forefathers' toil,
> He who commits this sin
> Will lead the estate to ruin.

CHAPTER XIII

An Appraisal

EVERY phase of the welfare program is highly controversial in Sweden: there are at least two conflicting viewpoints, and often more. There are those who consider that Sweden has gone far enough in social experimentation, if not too far. They think that it is time to call a halt. On the other hand, there are the progressives who want to push further and deliver more benefits to the people. They feel that there is always room for improvement, that the program cannot be static, and that the State should play an increasingly paternalistic role. These conflicts exist at all levels and particularly among those officials who have to formulate and carry out the welfare program.

The differences of opinion are resolved at intervals by a series of compromises, invariably in a progressive direction. Sweden may be called the land of compromise, for everything is settled by discussion and compromise, whether it be a major question of policy or an administrative issue at a low level. Everyone has his say and the majority decides.

The controversy over the program extends into all fields.

Consider, for instance, the co-operatives. The fundamental difference in viewpoints is between those who consider that the co-operatives render a valuable service to the nation by reducing the price of consumer goods and those who consider them to be a menace to free enterprise. But whatever side one may take in this controversy, the facts speak for themselves. The co-operatives are growing bigger and more influential with each passing year. In other words, the consumers are the determining factor. The trend is the same in every phase of the welfare program—the interest of the masses overrides that of the individual.

Housing is another controversial issue. The difference in this case is between those who advocate more control over housing and those who would get rid of the present restrictions and regulations. It might be thought that the people would be unanimous in seeking the removal of the restrictions and the restoration of a free building market. But there are many who feel that it is a primary duty of the State to provide adequate housing for the people and to play a paternalistic role. They do not seem to take into account that the State has so far failed to accomplish this by regulation. The emphasis for the future is on increased municipal and co-operative housing with Government support. This is a move in the same direction—away from private enterprise.

The new compulsory health insurance is the clearest evidence of the trend. For over twenty years there was a heated controversy between the advocates of compulsory health insurance and those who wanted to maintain the voluntary insurance system. The labor unions and some of the politicians were for free medicine, which was consistently and bitterly fought by the doctors. Their opposition was not based so much on principle as on practical considerations. They feared that compulsory health insurance would lower the standard of medical care, and they pointed to the shortage of doctors and nurses to cope with the added strain. But notwithstanding this opposition, Sweden moved toward free medicine by a series of compromises, inch by inch, until the last obstacle was overcome. The progressives won again, though it remains to be seen what sort of a victory it will be.

Child welfare is also a controversial problem. The big question is the extent to which authorities should have the right to intervene in the home. There are many social workers in Sweden who believe that the authorities should have even more power to step in and remove children from their homes if the parents are not caring for them properly than they have now. On the other hand, most parents believe that this should not be allowed and that no institutional care can adequately substitute for a home, however poor it may be. This issue is, for the moment, at the crossroads.

The same division exists on many other issues, such as the care of the aged. Are old people to be looked after by the State, or is it the obligation of relatives? The trend again is for the State to assume a more responsible role. In the matter of prison reform, it is the issue of the rehabilitation of the individual prisoner as against the protection of society. The attitude is toward more leniency for prisoners although crime is on the increase.

How far will Sweden continue in this progressive direction, and is there a danger that it will eventually lead to Communism?

That is a question I have asked of many Swedes in different walks of life, starting in first place with Prime Minister Tage Erlander. He says that the growing influence of the State in the life of the people is intended to bring freedom to them. Every Social Democratic politician, the Prime Minister affirms, believes fundamentally in a policy of freedom for the individual. "The more benefits you give the people," Erlander declares, "the more you increase their freedom and strengthen their resistance to Communism or any other form of dictatorship." The high standard of living which the Swedish State provides for the people, according to Erlander, is a guarantee against totalitarianism.

I asked the same question of Arne Lundberg, Undersecretary of State for Foreign Affairs, high in the Social Democratic hierarchy. He cannot foresee where the progressive trend will lead Sweden in the future, but he states categorically that there is no danger that it will lead to Communism, since no one in Sweden wants any kind of dictatorship. So long as the political parties are free and there are free elections and a free press, he says, no Swedish government can introduce reforms that would extinguish liberty. He believes that eventually there will be a stop to the social program or even a reversal, but he cannot predict when.

Many other Swedes with whom I have talked believe that the time cannot be far off. They are convinced that the limit has been reached as far as taxation to finance the welfare program is concerned. The benefits were welcome to the masses as long as the upper brackets were paying for them, but now that everyone is compelled to contribute his share, it is a different story, particularly with the expensive compulsory health insurance. Many Swedes believe that the Government has already committed itself too far and that a reaction is bound to set in and bring about that much talked about stop to socialization.

I questioned, among others, Ture Nerman, a reformed Communist who is now a bitter opponent of Communism in Parliament. He considers that a balance must be maintained between security and freedom and that the Government, in its search for security, has gone too far at the expense of freedom and too fast and that the taxes are now so high at all levels that the workers will be unwilling to pay for more benefits in the future.

I have not met a single Swede who feels that the welfare program will lead to Communism. On the contrary, most Swedes believe that the high standard of living prevailing in Sweden is an antidote to Communism. If any agitation should develop, it is more likely that it will take the form of a protest against the progressive trend. The Swedish people are well aware of the dangers of Communism. They know as well as any other free people what is going on behind the Iron Curtain, and they are as determined as any democratic country to maintain their independence.

Swedes are entitled to a whole series of benefits from the cradle to the grave—what the Social Democrats call a program for "security at all ages." These include prenatal care for expectant mothers, an allowance for a child at birth, an annual child subsidy, free dental care for children, free schoolbooks, free school lunches, loans for students, scholarships for more promising students, protective measures for workers, unemployment insurance, recreation facilities, loans for young married couples to furnish their homes, benefits for families such as reduced rentals, "own your home" building loans, free medical and surgical care in hospitals, low-rate outpatient care, pensions for invalids and the disabled, free annual vacations for housewives and children, and old-age pensions. Most of these benefits are available to all.

As a result of this comprehensive welfare program, there is in Sweden no destitution such as exists in so many other countries. There are no slums in the true sense of the word; no one has to sleep at night on a park bench or under a bridge; there is a high degree of security in employment; there is full employment; there are no beggars; there is a high standard of living for the people; and medical and hospital care is within the reach of everyone. This is an extraordinary achievement, of which the Swedish people may well be proud. Few nations can boast of such an impressive accomplishment. This is on the credit side.

But there is a debit side to the picture. The benefits have led to a complacency among the people which is the result of a secure living. There is no need to struggle for an existence. It is guaranteed by the State and the community. Initiative is blunted. This is due partly to the general well-being which eliminates some of the competitive urge, and also to the pressure of a meddling bureaucracy and the high taxation which discourages any incentive to strive for fortune. Some people feel that if the welfare is carried much further, it may bring about a change in the rugged individualistic character of the Swedish people, which would be molded to a pattern of uniformity.

Finance Minister Gunnar Sträng denies that the welfare program with its benefits has dulled the spirit of the Swedish people. He contends that it is only when people are freed from insecurity and anxiety that they are able to assert themselves creatively. "Independence and the will to work," he declares, "do not develop in a dependent situation and under the pressure of fear and want." This is a very debatable argument, for genius and creative stimulus only too often spring from conditions of abject poverty and adversity.

On the other hand, Jarl Hjalmarsson, leader of the Conservative opposition party, says, "What we need in Sweden is a plan for economic freedom and not a policy to control the unfavorable consequences of regulation."

But on balance the welfare program has worked admirably for Sweden. There has been no long-range planning, but it has been carried out step by step, often by trial and error. In a small country such as Sweden, if an experiment fails, it can be set aside without too serious consequences, and something else substituted. It is clear to any visitor that Sweden is a prosperous, orderly, well administered country with a clean

political record and a minimum of corruption among official-
dom.

The Swedes realize that their small neutral country would
be at the mercy of the big powers in the event of a third
world war with atomic weapons. That is, of course, what they
fear most. But if providence will spare them this fate and
they can continue to concentrate on their own affairs, the
future of the welfare program will remain in the hands of the
voters. The Swedish people have the opportunity to express
themselves in free elections every other year. Public opinion
is stable and there are no sensational changes, but politicians
are extremely sensitive to even small fluctuations. The voters
can give the program the red or green light at any time. Thus
a proud, resolute people determine their own destiny, but
they do not say that the way they have chosen is for others.

Acknowledgments

In the course of several years of intensive study and preparation of material for this book, I came into contact with hundreds of persons identified in one way or another with the Swedish welfare program. It would be impossible to list all of them here, but I would be remiss if I did not mention some of those who gave so freely and patiently of their time to discuss with me the many phases of a complicated subject.

I had the opportunity to meet the late King, Gustav V, and the present King, Gustav VI Adolph, and to learn of his conception of the duties of a democratic sovereign in a world where kings and royal households have become scarce. I was also privileged to see the King's own famous collection of Chinese antiquities and to hear him explain the historic background of some of the rarer specimens.

I interviewed many officials connected with the administration of the welfare program, including Prime Minister Tage Erlander, who is also head of the Social Democratic Party; Gustav Möller, who was for over a score of years Minister of Social Welfare and who probably knows the subject more intimately than any other Swede; Möller's wife,

Else Kleen; Gunnar Hedlund, Minister of the Interior and head of the Farmers' Party; Arne Lundberg, Under Secretary of State for Foreign Affairs; Axel Strand, head of the powerful Federation of Labor and Deputy Speaker in the First Chamber of parliament; Richard Sterner, one of the authors of the Social Democratic Party platform and a former delegate at the United Nations; Ture Nerman, prominent member of parliament; Lars Axelsson, head of the Tax-Payers Association; Gustav Holmstedt, statistician in the Bureau of the Budget.

Also: Ernst Bexelius, director general of the Social Welfare Board; Konrad Persson, director general of the Pensions Board; Karl Erik Granath, director of the Child Welfare Board in Stockholm; Hugo Nilsson, superintendent of Sabbatsberg old-age home; Harry Biltberg, superintendent of Rosenlund old-age home; Ivar Lidman, superintendent of the Nyboda home for children; Miss Christian Ellwyn, of the Social Welfare Board and a former delegate at the United Nations; Karl Axel Anell, director general of the Crown Lands Board; Wilhelm Plym-Forschell, director general of the Board of Forestry; and Karl Höjer, former director general of the Social Welfare Board.

In my study of the relationship between government and big business, I talked with many of Sweden's top industrial leaders and bankers, including: Axel Enström, managing director of Cellulosa, Sweden's largest timber industry, and chairman of the Employers' Association; Kurt Söderberg, Vice President of the Association of Swedish Industries; Stig Odeen, former chairman of the wartime Production Board; Tore Browald, head of the Employees' Association; Kuno Möller, President of the Margarine Company; Hjalmar Aselius, managing director of Fagersta iron mines; Erland Waldenström, managing director of TGO, the Grängesberg iron ore mines; Baron Gerard de Geer, member of parliament and leading industrialist; Tor Bonnier, head of the Bonnier Publishing House; Jacob Wallenberg, banker; Rolf Kalissendorf, Wallenberg's right hand man in the Enskilda Bank; Tage Wärn, former President of the Bankers' Association; Clas Boman, Secretary of the Food Products Association; Jonas Nordensson, of the Industrial Investigation Institute; Arne Skarby, Vice President of the Federation of Private Retailers; Herbert Kastengren, President of Phillips Lamps; Hugo Åberg, chief accountant for the Grängesberg mines; G. R. Broms, son of the mining pioneer; and Charles Cederholm of the Water Power Board.

My inquiry into the workings of the co-operatives stretched over several years and brought me into contact with Albin Johansson, Chairman of the Board, who opened the doors wide for me and enabled me to look into every phase of the movement; Martin Bonow, Vice Chairman of the Board, a model of efficiency; and all the other members of the Board individually. I also interviewed many of the chiefs of sections and lesser executives. I am especially grateful to Miss Sally Frolich, Mr. Johansson's able secretary who arranged many of the interviews for me and who was always most helpful. Among others in the co-operative movement who assisted me were: Herman Stolpe, head of the Co-operative Publishing Company; Nils Thedin, editor of *Vi*, magazine of the co-operatives; Professor Gunnar Silverstolpe, author and authority on the co-operatives; Harald Elldin, head of the Co-operative Training School; Hjalmar Ohlson, who runs the Gustavsberg porcelain factory, and the three famous artists; Ivar Kåge, Stig Lindberg and Berndt Friberg. Also the cordial and enthusiastic Einar Sjögren, chairman of the Federation of Swedish Farmers' Associations, the big rural co-operative organization.

I discussed the controversial medical program with a long list of doctors, nurses, social curators and patients, in and out of hospitals. Among them were: Dr. Arthur Engel, director general of the Royal Medical Board; Dr. Dag Knutsson, head of the Doctors' Association; Dr. Olof Johansson, chairman of the Young Doctors' Association; Dr. Verner Westberg, head of St. Erik's Hospital; Dr. Erik Groth of the Royal Medical Board; Dr. Helge Knoos, head of Psychiatric Hospital; Dr. Axel Höjer, former director general of the Royal Medical Board; Professor Gustav Nylin, heart specialist and section chief at Southern Hospital; Rolf Broberg, secretary of two committees which drafted the medical program; Miss Gerda Höjer, President of the Nurses' Association; the Misses Elizabeth Bergsten and Janny-Lisa Olsson, social curators at Southern Hospital; the late Hjalmar Cederström, the architect who built Southern Hospital; and Åke Natt och Dag, director general of the Government Insurance Agency which finances the compulsory health insurance.

In my investigation of prison reform, I interviewed, among others, Hardy Göransson, director of prisons; Torsten Eriksson, a leading official of the Department of Justice who has attended many conferences abroad as Sweden's representative; Lennart Asplund, Stockholm Public Procurator; Gerhard Bostedt, assistant director of Långholmen Prison; Harry Gibbling, of the Board of Youth Prisons; Harry Widemyr, a devoted social worker; Mrs. Ingrid Gärde Widemar and Miss Valborg Lundgren, both prominent women lawyers and members of parliament; Baroness Ruth Stjernstedt, lawyer; and Curt Falkenstam, veteran crime reporter on *Svenska Dagbladet*, who put me on the track of several criminal cases.

Others to whom I am indebted include: Kåge Ehrbacke, vice chief of the Liquor System; Harry Brynielsson, managing director of the Atomic Energy Company; Justus Gustavsson, director of the Housing Board; Olle Engkvist, architect and contractor; Nils Olof Nässtrom and Åke Johnson of the Cooperative Housing Association; Count Stephen Wachmeister, owner of Bogesund estate; and Ingemar Hägglöf, delegate at the OEEC in Paris.

To Professor Bertil Ohlin, leader of the Liberal opposition party, a middle-of-the-roader, I am especially indebted for looking over my manuscript and for his helpful suggestions.

My thanks to Walton Butterworth, former American Ambassador to Sweden, for his advice and encouragement, and other Embassy officials, including Marshall Green, DuWayne G. Clark and Paul Du Vivier.

Finally, a word of gratitude to my wife, Greta, and to the immediate members of my family who shared this experience with me and lent their counsel.

W. F.

Index